HOW TO NEGOTIATE A LEASE ON YOUR TERMS

GUERILLA TACTICS FOR RENTING AN APARTMENT, HOUSE OR TRAILER HOME.

Now you can know what rights you as a tenant have.

Information that your landlord will never tell you.

How to break a lease without being held liable.

A checklist to inspect the premises is included.

How to make sure you get back your security deposit.

Know the same information on the law that your landlord knows. Know your rights before and after you sign a lease.

Almost every single detail that is written in a lease is for the benefit of the landlord. Do you know how to protect yourself?

Now you can learn how by using the most authoritative book ever written in English (not legalese) for your protection.

Landlords will read this book to find out what you know and how to negotiate with you.

VALID IN ALL 50 STATES

written by **David Waldman, Esq.**   ISBN #1879191-00-2   Copyright 1991 — David Waldman
A Lawyer who has 1st hand experience in the Landlord to Tenant Experience.

GREETINGS FROM THE AUTHOR

Congratulations on buying **Lease On Your Terms.** This book is designed to acquaint you with residential leases for apartments, condominiums, private houses and mobile homes. This book will also introduce you to the way landlords think.

MOST IMPORTANTLY, **LEASE ON YOUR TERMS** PROVIDES PRE-PRINTED FORMS WHICH ENABLE YOU TO OFFER THE LANDLORD YOUR PROPOSED CHANGES TO THE LANDLORD'S FORM OF THE LEASE.

We have used our best efforts to compile forms containing accurate, complete and easy to understand information. We believe that the terms set forth in the forms will be understood by the legal and business people with whom you will be dealing on the other side of the transaction.

We do not guarantee that the way you fill in or use the forms in this book will be correct and complete for you in your circumstances. You will be best served by having an attorney, who is familiar with your personal affairs and knowledgeable about your legal options, review your strategy and actual use of the completed form.

The forms exist for your informational purposes and the author of this book is not acting as your personal attorney.

We have made our best efforts to provide you with clear instructions and forms that will allow you to learn about remedies and procedures you are administering through your own program of self-help.

WHEN USING THE FORMS IN THIS BOOK, YOU ARE ACTING AS YOUR OWN ATTORNEY. THE AUTHOR, PUBLISHER, DISTRIBUTOR AND SELLERS OF THIS BOOK AND THEIR ASSOCIATES **ARE NOT LIABLE** FOR THE MATERIAL INCLUDED IN THIS BOOK OR FOR YOUR USE OF THOSE MATERIALS. THE USE OF THIS BOOK AND FORMS CONSTITUTES A WAIVER BY THE BUYER OR USER OF THIS BOOK OF ALL LIABILITY AGAINST THE AUTHOR, PUBLISHER, DISTRIBUTOR OR SELLERS OF THIS BOOK.

This book does not cover everything. No single book can. Everything is too much to include in a practical "how to book".

Use your brain and God given sense to fill in the gaps of knowledge or consult with professionals.

WARNING

1. Law is a compiliation of Federal, state, county, city and local statutes, rules, court decisions and opinions of various Attorneys General and regulatory bodies. Sometimes even judges do not agree on the law.

2.. You may interpret statements in this book incorrectly.

3. You may fill in the FORMS incorrectly.

4. The law may change after this book is printed. This book may now be wrong.

5. The law may be different where you reside.

USE THIS BOOK AT YOUR OWN RISK; THERE IS NO GUARANTY OR WARRANTY EXPRESSED OR IMPLIED. USE, ENJOY AND PROFIT FROM THIS BOOK.

TABLE OF CONTENTS

INTRODUCTION

A VERITABLE SURVIVAL MANUAL FOR TENANTS.

GET EVEN WITH YOUR LANDLORD WHEN YOU NEGOTIATE YOUR LEASE; IT'S TOO LATE TO GET EVEN AFTER YOUR SIGN A DEAD END LEASE.

AN ABSOLUTE NECESSITY IN TODAY'S CHANGING MARKET.

LEASE ON YOUR TERMS APPLIES TO RENTALS OF ANY RESIDENCE INCLUDING APARTMENTS, MOBILE HOMES AND PRIVATE HOMES.

NEVER AGAIN ENTER A RESIDENTIAL LEASE AT A COMPETITIVE DISADVANTAGE. EQUALIZE THE BARGAINING PROCESS WITH **LEASE ON YOUR TERMS**.

EXPLOIT THE DECLINING REAL ESTATE MARKET; TAKE ADVANTAGE OF YOUR ENHANCED BARGAINING POSITION.

DON'T BE A VICTIM OF LANDLORDS| FIGHT BACK NOW.

LANDLORD TENANT LAW HAS BEEN ALTERED IN THE TENANT'S FAVOR IN THE LAST DECADE. **LEASE ON YOUR TERMS** ADVISES YOU OF THESE CHANGES IN YOUR FAVOR.

GET DECENT LIVING CONDITIONS AT AFFORDABLE PRICES.

FIND OUT WHY EVERYONE HATES A LANDLORD AND WHAT YOU CAN DO TO PROTECT YOURSELF.

ARM YOURSELF WITH THE LATEST AND BEST TENANT'S LEASE CLAUSES WHEN YOU DEAL WITH YOUR LANDLORD.

YOUR LANDLORD SPENDS THOUSANDS OF DOLLARS FOR LEGAL ADVISE TO USE AGAINST YOU| SHOULDN'T YOU SPEND A FEW DOLLARS IN SELF DEFENSE IN ORDER TO BE ONE STEP AHEAD OF YOUR LANDLORD?

EXPLODES WITH SAGE ADVICE THAT MORE THAN PAYS FOR THE COST OF THE BOOK.

NO LONGER DOES YOUR RESIDENTIAL LEASE HAVE TO BE A ONE-SIDED DOCUMENT DRAFTED BY YOUR LANDLORD AND FOR YOUR LANDLORD.

LEASE ON YOUR TERMS IS THE BIG EQUALIZER; LEASE ON YOUR TERMS IS TO RESIDENTIAL LEASES WHAT THE SIX SHOOTER WAS TO THE OLD WEST.

NEVER AGAIN GO UNREPRESENTED.

SAVE MUCH MORE THAN THE PRICE OF THIS BOOK IN RENTAL BENEFITS.

THE STANDARD FORM OF RESIDENTIAL LEASE

The only feature that is standard on the standard form of apartment lease in your state is that the **standard form of residential lease is written by the landlord interests for the landlord interests.**

ARM YOURSELF WITH LEASE ON YOUR TERMS

Everyone knows that the residential lease is weighted heavily in the landlord's favor. There isn't much in the lease offered by the landlord that helps the tenant. Mere possession of the rented premises is all the tenant receives in exchange for all of the legal obligations the tenant undertakes.

At least be armed with **Lease On Your Terms** and its ammunition of TENANT'S RIDERS. This book will show you how to negotiate with your landlord in terms he understands. It will also furnish your pre-printed changes to the lease.

The book will also give you valuable insight into the landlord's thought process. It will show you what changes to the lease are acceptable to the landlord.

WRITTEN BY A SKILLED LAWYER TO HELP YOU

Lease On Your Terms was written by a lawyer skilled in the art of negotiating and drafting residential leases. Most people cannot afford to hire an attorney to review, negotiate and draft a lease for their residence. Therefore, most tenants are not receiving effective representation when they are most in need of advice.

Landlords, on the other hand, are extremely well represented. And tenants are made acutely aware of it. The real estate system was sculptured by landlords for the exclusive benefit of the landed interests.

WHY EVERYBODY HATES A LANDLORD

Nobody likes a landlord. Landlords even hate each other. The reason no one likes a landlord is that they hold all the high cards in the legal deck.

From time to time landlords have to sue in court in order to enforce their manifold and powerful rights granted to them in the lease. WHEN LANDLORDS SUE, THEY USUALLY WIN.

Landlords win in court because most of the provisions of the lease are drafted in their favor. The lease provisions have been drafted by expensive, talented and dedicated lawyers, many of whom are themselves landlords and are driven by the self motivation underlying the Arab proverb that only the eye of an owner can fatten up a camel. The landlord oriented lease terms have been refined by years of trial and error. As a result only those clauses most likely to benefit the landlords have survived. This perpetuates a Darwinistic survival of only the fittest of the legal clauses best designed to help the landlord.

Landlords also win in court because the long history of the common law of England was written and interpreted by the landed gentry who were both the landlords and the judges.

WHO NEEDS THE TENANT'S GUIDE?

A survey conducted in the early 1970s generally indicated that one-third of the people in the United States lived in rented housing. By 1990 that number had increased. According to the U.S. Bureau of the Census Statistical Abstract of the United States: 1990 (110th Edition), 36.1 percent of the current population of the United States lives in renter occupied housing.

Actually, 36.1 percent is a very conservative figure because it does not adequately reflect the larger families among the poor, the failure to include all poor families in census reports and the failure to account for families doubling up for lack of housing.

According to a recent 1991 article in THE NEW YORK TIMES the percentage of owner-occupied dwellings in New York City increased from 15% in 1940 to 28% in 1990. This still means that 72% of the people living in New York City are renting.

HOW MANY PEOPLE RENT?

One recent publication talking only about apartments concluded that over 70 million Americans are apartment dwellers representing 3/5 of the non-white population and 1/3 of the white population. This does not include renters of mobile homes and private homes.

According to the U.S. Bureau of the Census Statistical Abstract of the United States: 1990 (110th Edition), in 1988, 32,852,000 households in the United States lived in renter occupied housing. The number of people in each household averaged 2.2 persons according to that same source. This means that at least 72,274402 people lived in renter occupied housing in 1988.

RENTING IS A WAY OF LIFE

Renting is an economic necessity to both tenants and landlords. According to the 1990 United States Government census, only nine percent of the people living in rental units can afford to buy houses.

The U.S. Bureau of the Census Statistical Abstract of the United States: 1990 (110th Edition) states that over 42 billion dollars was loaned by institutional lenders for multifamily residential construction loans in 1987. During 1987 according to that same source over 207 billion dollars was loaned by those same institutional lenders for long-term mortgages on multifamily residential properties. Any way you look at it, 247 billion dollars of financing in one year denotes the size of the residential real estate market.

Renting is reality. Renting will exist as a method of living for tenants and a method of doing business for landlords for many years. Prudence dictates that you as a tenant learn all you can. The wisdom you glean from **Lease On Your Terms** will pay huge dividends to you for many years.

WHY A TENANT'S GUIDE TO RESIDENTIAL LEASES?

This book is written in simple plain English to give residential tenants the knowledge and ability to understand, negotiate and prepare a suitable and livable lease for their residence. It is written specifically for tenants. **Lease On Your Terms** covers most standard clauses in your residential lease and explains what the clause means to you and your landlord.

Moreover, **Lease On Your Terms** offers valuable tenant's oriented changes to counter the landlord's standard lease. These tenant's changes are pre-printed for your convenience on pages which can be detached from the book and be presented to the landlord as your proposed tenant's clauses to the lease.

MOST IMPORTANTLY, **LEASE ON YOUR TERMS** HAS TYPED YOUR PROPOSED CHANGES AS PRE-PRINTED TENANT'S RIDERS TO THE LANDLORD ORIENTED LEASE OFFERED TO YOU BY YOUR LANDLORD. EACH PROPOSED TENANT'S CLAUSE WHICH YOU WANT TO INCLUDE IN YOUR VERSION OF THE LEASE CAN BE OFFERED TO THE LANDLORD AS PART OF THE NEGOTIATING PROCESS.

THE NEGOTIATION ZONE

After you have given your proposed changes to the lease to the landlord, you and the landlord are on equal footing. **Lease On Your Terms** equalizes the knowledge between you and your landlord. **Lease On Your Terms** gives you valuable insight into those lease changes to which you are entitled and the landlord should accept.

You are then in a negotiation zone where each of you and the landlord negotiate for those clauses which you need and trade off other rights neither of you really need. **Lease On Your Terms** will also teach you how to negotiate each proposed change.

THE LANDLORD LOBBY

Landlords have always organized into real estate associations, builder owner associations and other such groups for their mutual comfort and aggrandizement. They meet, eat three martini lunches and teach each other new tricks.

These associations have lobbyists in Washington D.C. and each state capital in order to protect landlord interests. They also have the financial heft to finance elections of legislators and judges sympathetic to their interests.

YOU AND YOUR LEASE

Surely you would agree that a man's home is his castle and that the lease which touches so intently upon your mode and manner of living is one of the most important relationship documents that you ever sign. Not only does the lease affect your life style, but it also places affirmative obligations upon you.

YOU HAVE A RIGHT TO USE AND ENJOY YOUR RESIDENCE. You wouldn't think so after a strict reading of the lease and its restrictions. **Lease On Your Terms** will highlight the rights you and your guests have to use and enjoy your rented dwelling.

HISTORICAL PAST

In the English common law (upon which our American system of jurisprudence is based) the owner of the land was the lord of the land. The basic principle was that the lord of the land could control all of his tenant's activities and the tenant was a powerless vassal and a villain to boot. The landlord even had the privilege under common law of first night rights to sleep with the peasant's bride. Needless to say, the landlord-tenant relationship was rife with discord and class hatred.

Few would want to return to those days of yesteryear. Most would agree that such feudal thinking has no place in the modern world.

TYPES OF TENANCIES

In Robin Hood's time most tenancies were "at will" tenancies. The tenant could occupy the land at the landlord's "will". The landlord could dispossess the tenant at any time for any reason or for no reason. A tenant held land at the good pleasure of the landlord.

This "at will" length of the lease didn't help the landlord or the tenant. Tenant's were loath to plant someone else's field and be evicted the day before the harvest. Landlords finally figured that yearly leases would be more productive.

In most jurisdictions, a month to month tenant must give thirty days advance notice to vacate the premises. The year to year tenant can move at the end of the year. You must check each of your (i) lease, (ii) state and (iii) municipal law on the amount of notice required before you can move out.

More tenant oriented states like New York and New Jersey have evolved from periodic tenancies (month to month or year to year) into tenancies regulated by statutes. New York City has its famous rent control and rent stabilization laws. New Jersey has an Eviction For Good Cause Act under which the landlord must renew the tenant's lease unless the landlord can establish good cause why the tenant should be evicted.

Lease On Your Terms has included a Notice Of Intention To Vacate Form set forth below.

TENANT'S NOTICE OF INTENTION TO VACATE FORM

To: _____

_____

_____

Date:_____

Re: Tenant's notice of intention to vacate premises
Reference is made to premises known as_____

_____

_____.

Please take notice that the undersigned tenant(s) will vacate the premises
on_____.

In accordance with the lease the tenant's security deposit should be returned

_____

_____

Please forward mail to the following forwarding address:

_____

_____

_____

_____
Tenant

_____
Tenant

   Mailed certified mail return receipt requested with a second copy mailed first class mail in a postage prepaid properly addressed envelope; or Delivered by Hand:

RECEIVED_____
Landlord or agent

Date:_____

RECENT DEVELOPMENTS IN LAW

Most people today agree that the common law view of the landed gentry versus the disenfranchised peasant is outdated and unworkable. It is also contrary to the twentieth century world and current thinking.

Recent developments in the law greatly favor tenants. Tenants are making big gains in their rights. The courts and legislatures have begun to realize that the old landlord—tenant law was poorly adapted to the needs of tenants and have been making landmark and benchmark changes in order to more equalize the relationship.

Some legislators have even begun to realize that tenants have the right to vote. And as Abraham Lincoln realized, God prefers poor people to rich people; that's why he made so many more of them. This gives tenant's the right to vote the rascals out of office. For this reason legislatures as a whole have begun to listen to tenant's needs.

A few of the major changes are listed below:

1. Tenants can now sue landlords where such a suit at common law would have ended the lease.

2. Landlords' non-responsibility for on premises accidents and robberies is being chipped away.

3. Retaliatory evictions for exercise of tenants' rights should now be over in most states.

4. Tenants are entitled to a warranty of habitability which means that the rented premises must be suitable for human habitation.

Regrettably these decisions vary from state to state and from city to city. **Lease On Your Terms** cannot and does not purport to list the landlord tenant laws of all of the states and municipalities in the United States. Instead **Lease On Your Terms** handles matters on a consensual basis. You and your landlord can agree to any changes in the lease that are lawful in your jurisdiction. The agreed to tenant's changes are added to the lease by means of the tenant's riders.

LIVE LEGAL COUNSEL CAN'T HURT

Lease On Your Terms recommends that if you can afford the fees, hire a real live attorney to review, negotiate and draft changes to the lease for your home. **Lease On Your Terms** is not a substitute for aggressive and sage legal advice. Words and their meaning as interpreted by courts can be dangerous. Socrates may have lived for another seventy years had his words not been deemed blasphemous and corruptive of the youth of Athens.

You should certainly consult with an attorney, if you get served with legal papers for your eviction from your rented premises. You may have a defense you haven't even considered. Furthermore, a good lawyer may even find that you have a case against your landlord entitling you to recover money from the landlord.

LEASE ON YOUR TERMS IS HELPFUL BUT WHEN YOU DON'T KNOW EXACTLY WHAT TO DO OR THE EXPENSIVE CHIPS ARE DOWN, THE PERSON WHO REPRESENTS HIMSELF HAS A FOOL FOR A LAWYER AND A FOOL FOR A CLIENT.

USE LEASE ON YOUR TERMS SELECTIVELY

Lease On Your Terms has much more information than you will need in order to negotiate a lease that you can live with happily. If anything, there is probably too much ammunition for you in this book.

You must analyze your needs and chose only those clauses that will help. Don't overwhelm your landlord with all the riders as tenant's proposed changes. Only select those riders you actually need in order to counter the landlord's written lease and to achieve your goals.

YOU MUST READ THE LANDLORD'S LEASE AND DO A LAWYER-LIKE JOB OF WEIGHING EACH OF YOUR PROPOSED CHANGES AGAINST YOUR RELATIVE BARGAINING POSITION AND YOUR NEEDS.

THE BATTLE OF THE FORMS

You will be armed with the Tenant oriented forms set forth in the FORMS section of **Lease On Your Terms**. These forms will help you through most of the rental transaction. From time to time you will meet a landlord who has his own forms. This is especially true of a large institutional landlord.

You now have a Mexican standoff. You have your forms and the landlord has his forms. What do you do? Read the forms. There is no magic in which form you use. It is the words on the forms that are important. Read both forms and negotiate for the provisions that help you.

Lease On Your Terms contains tenant oriented forms. The landlord's forms will be landlord oriented as much as the law allows and then some. You may even have thought of a better clause more suited to your needs than is contained in either set of forms. Negotiate for the terms that set forth the substance of the deal and that most favor you. You are bounded only by your bargaining power.

THE REALLY IMPORTANT CLAUSES

Not all clauses in the tenant's proposed riders are essential for your needs. Only you can assess your needs and be in a position to know your true financial, emotional and physical person. For example, if you are facing a job transfer to a different city in the near but indefinite future, you must have the right to sublet or assign the lease to a new tenant. Otherwise, you could be liable for the rent after you vacate without the right to help yourself by finding a replacement tenant.

A short list of the more important tenant's clauses to be inserted as riders to the lease are set forth below in order of relative importance.

1. Tenant's Sublease Clause, or
2. Tenant's Assignment Clause
3. Tenant's Security Deposit Clause
4. Tenant's Move-In Clause
5. Tenant's Delivery of the Premises Clause
6. Such other clauses as you deem necessary to protect your special needs and interests.

ORGANIZATION OF MATERIAL IN LEASE ON YOUR TERMS

Lease On Your Terms has noticed several distinct problem areas concerning residential leases. These problem areas are divided on a transactional basis as follows:

PART 1 — Pre-lease problems

PART 2 — Problems of inspecting the premises

PART 3 — Negotiating for your changes to the landlord's form lease

PART 4 — Moving-in problems

PART 5 — Living under the lease

PART 6 — Lease renewal

PART 7 — Moving-out problems

PART 8 — Mobile home parks

PART 9 — Your Tenant's miscellaneous legal changes to be added as riders to the landlord's standard lease

PART 10— THE FORMS

Accordingly **Lease On Your Terms** will divided into sub-parts in order to make each problem easier to deal with as the rich tapestry of the rental transaction unfolds.

PART 1

PRE-LEASE PROBLEMS

TRUTH IN RENTING LAW

In many states the form leases that are offered to tenants do not accurately reflect the state of the law which may have changed in the tenant's favor. Although in many jurisdictions recent laws and court cases have imposed upon landlord's numerous obligations such as the implied warranty of habitability and eviction only for just cause (as in New Jersey), form leases either ignored or sought to absolve the landlord from these obligations.

New Jersey, for example, has passed a Truth in Renting Law which prohibits a landlord from offering or entering into a written lease "which included a lease provision which violates clearly established legal rights of tenants or responsibilities of landlords as established by the law of this State at the time the lease is signed."

As a result of the Truth in Renting Law, the tenant has a statutory right to a lease which accurately sets forth the law. Without a Truth in Renting Law you may well get a deceptive lease that misstates your rights and liabilities.

Many states and cities do not have a Truth in Renting Law. As a result there may well be unenforceable provisions in your lease that you do not know about. There may also be landlord oriented clauses that attempt to shield the landlord from his legal responsibilities to you. The clauses are buried in the lease by the landlord or his attorneys. They hope to intimidate you into yielding if you discover a legitimate grievance. The landlord plans to show where you have "waived" this right in the very lease you signed.

Phoney, pseudo and unlawful waivers and other unenforceable clauses are knowingly inserted in leases by disreputable landlord interests for what lawyers call the "in terrorem" (in terror) chilling effect which the clause tends to have on the actions of the uneducated. Fortunately, **Lease On Your Terms** will help to remove the fangs from most of these snakes.

PLAIN ENGLISH LEASES

Under New York State law leases for residential property have to be written in plain English. This means language that is understandable and comprehensible to the average lay person. Until the "plain English" law was passed, leases were written in lawyer's legalese with confusing terms like "party of the first part" (instead of landlord) and "party of the second part" (instead of your identification as tenant). Leases used to abound with "wherefores", "hereinafters", "anything herein or elsewhere to the contrary notwithstanding" and the like.

It may very well be that the state in which you live does not have a plain English law. Plain English will make the lease more understandable to you. **Lease On Your Terms** will help you decipher legalese and walk away with a lease best suited to your needs and your relative bargaining position.

LANDLORD'S RESTRICTIONS ON USE AND OCCUPANCY
- OR -
CAN I RUN MY BUSINESS OUT OF MY RESIDENCE?
- OR -
HOW MANY PEOPLE CAN LIVE IN ONE DWELLING?

The Use Clause

Your lease will have a use clause. The use clause will state that you shall use the residence for living purposes only.

If you want to use your residence as an office, you must modify the use clause to state that you may use the residence as an office for your "typing service" or such other business as you may wish to conduct.

It is probably best to state that you may use the residence for "an office" in broad and general terms so that you can change your line of work without having to obtain the landlord's additional consent.

The Occupancy Clause

Your lease will have an Occupancy Clause. The Occupancy Clause states who has authority to live in the dwelling. The Occupancy Clause is the landlord's attempt to limit who can live in the dwelling by name, number of persons or family relationship.

A typical landlord's Occupancy Clause will provide as follows:

"Tenant shall use the apartment for living purposes only. The apartment may be occupied by the tenant or tenants named above and by the immediate family of the tenant or tenants."

Under New York law, for example, it is unlawful for a landlord to restrict occupancy of residential premises, by lease terms or otherwise, to a tenant or

tenants or to tenants and their immediate family. This law protects tenants from being evicted as a result of their economic need to share living quarters with nonfamily members. It also protects your right of association to live with anyone you wish.

New York State law allows an apartment to be occupied by the tenant, by the immediate family of the tenant, and by one additional occupant and the dependant children of the occupant. This is a very heavy density.

Unless local housing regulations state otherwise, a landlord is free to adopt reasonable guidelines for occupancy as long as the rules are applied consistently and evenly to all applicants. The rule of thumb used by many landlords is one fewer occupant than the number of rooms. The landlord may limit efficiency dwellings to one person, one bedrooms to two, two bedrooms to three and so on. Exceeding this population density increases the landlord's maintenance and repair costs considerably. The dwelling takes more abuse, more use and wears out more quickly.

As you would expect the United States Department of Housing and Urban Development increases the population density allowed in their units for public housing. Its maximums and minimums for rental occupancy are as follows:

Efficiency (no bedrooms)	one to two occupants
One Bedroom	one to three occupants
Two Bedrooms	two to five occupants
Three Bedrooms	three to seven occupants
Four Bedrooms	six to nine occupants

The landlord walks a delicate balance. He is not able to discriminate in certain prejudice oriented ways (see below). Yet when selecting tenants his natural desire is to be discriminating in a business oriented manner. He wants to attract the best possible tenants who will augment the landlord's investment.

Under New York law the tenant must inform the landlord of the name of any occupant within 30 days following the commencement of occupancy or within 30 days following a request by the landlord. AN OCCUPANT DOES NOT ACQUIRE THE RIGHT OR LIABILITIES OF A TENANT.

The reason for giving notice to the landlord is to invoke the protective rights of occupancy of the occupant.

Lease On Your Terms has included an Identity of New Occupant Form below and in the FORMS section of this book.

IDENTITY OF NEW OCCUPANT FORM

_____
Insert Date

Re: Notification of New Occupant

_____
Insert name of Landlord

_____
Insert landlord's street address

_____
Insert landlord's city, state and zip code

Dear Landlord:

Reference is made to the lease between you and the undersigned for the premises set forth below. Please be advised that the person(s) listed below will be additional occupants of the premises rented from you by the undersigned.

NAME(S) OF ADDITIONAL OCCUPANT(S)

_____

_____

_____

_____

Very truly yours,

_____
Insert your name(s) as on the lease

_____
Insert your street address

_____
Insert your City, State and Zip Code

IMPORTANT NOTE: BE CERTAIN THAT YOU ARE AUTHORIZED AN ADDITIONAL OCCUPANT BEFORE YOU SEND THIS NOTICE TO THE LANDLORD. REREAD THE ABOVE SECTION OF **LEASE ON YOUR TERMS** CONCERNING HOW MANY PEOPLE CAN LIVE IN ONE DWELLING.

DISCRIMINATION IN RENTING

OVERVIEW

In the absence of a constitutional or statutory prohibition, a private landlord is free to be as arbitrary or capricious as he pleases in determining to whom he will rent.

A number of statutes on the Federal, State and Municipal levels do limit the landlord's freedom of choice. Among them are prohibitions against discrimination on the basis of race, creed, national origin, age, sex, sexual orientation or preferences and the presence of children.

Regrettably, it is beyond the purview of this book to report upon the patchwork of individual state and local laws preventing discrimination. Accordingly, the reader is advised to use this short narrative section as springboard to further individual research to protect your rights.

Until the Equal Rights Amendment to the U.S. Constitution is passed, a single law on many of these issues will not exist.

DISCRIMINATION BASED ON RACE, CREED, NATIONAL ORIGIN OR ANCESTRY

FEDERAL LAW

There are Federal laws prohibiting landlords from discriminating on the basis of race, creed, national origin or ancestry. These laws are referred to as the Civil Rights Act of 1968, the Federal Fair Housing Act, and the Fair Housing Amendments Act of 1988.

STATE LAWS

There are also similar State laws in New Jersey and in New York. Under these laws there are no exceptions; the prohibition is applicable to all landlords. There may also be local state or municipal laws preventing discrimination where you live.

THE STRONGEST CIVIL RIGHTS BILL IN THE NATION

The New York City Council in 1991 passed one of the strongest laws in the nation prohibiting discrimination in housing, employment and public accommodations. The bill reaches further than existing city law to protect New Yorkers from discrimination and offer them legal and financial remedies. For instance, the old New York City law did not prohibit age bias in residential housing or discrimination in two-family, owner occupied dwellings where an available apartment had been publicly advertised. The new law outlaws both forms of bias.

Nor did the old law provided for any civil penalties in discrimination cases. Under the old law, people who felt they had been discriminated against had to take their grievances to the city's Human Rights Commission. Under the new law, they would be allowed to go to the Commission or the State Supreme Court.

The new law permits civil penalties of up to $250,000 in cases of systemic discrimination.

The bill, jointly shaped by Mayor David Dinkens and the Council, was meant to send a strong signal to Washington where Congress was grappling with the language of a civil rights bill. New York City's Corporation Counsel stated, "It is fair to say that our law will be one of the strongest, if not the strongest, in the nation."

The New York City bill includes gay people as a protected class unlike New York State or Federal law. New York City now has tougher laws than the Federal Government for protection for people.

In language aimed at protecting gay people or people with AIDS, the law would prohibit discrimination based on perceived membership in a group or association with someone in a protected group.

METHODS, MEANS AND INDICIA OF DISCRIMINATION

Discrimination can occur not only through outright rejection, but also by tactics of discouragement such as by delay, credit investigations, withholding of material information, or by subtle suggestions that the applicant is unwelcome.

Discrimination is invidious and creeps into renting in many ways. The landlord can refuse to show the apartment, tell you the apartment is already rented or can enormously inflate the rent or security deposit above what you can afford.

GAY RIGHTS

In some states and municipalities it is also against the law to reject prospective renters on the basis of sex or sexual preference. New York City but not New York State has legislation barring discrimination on the basis of sexual preference. The Connecticut legislature in 1991 passed a bill which the governor was expected to sign which bars discrimination in housing against homosexuals. You should check with a women's rights or gay rights group in your area in order to discover the effectiveness of city and state laws in your area.

DISCRIMINATION AGAINST CHILDREN

Under New York State law it is a misdemeanor to discriminate against children in dwelling houses or mobile home parks. More specifically, it is illegal to discriminate in the terms, conditions, or privileges of any such rental, solely on the ground that such person or family has or have a child or children.

The prohibition against discrimination against children in dwelling houses and mobile home parks does not apply to:

1. housing units for senior citizens subsidized, insured, or guaranteed by the federal government; or

2. one or two family owner occupied dwelling houses or mobile homes; or

3. mobile home parks exclusively for persons fifty-five years of age or older.

Furthermore, under New York State law it is illegal to provide in a lease that the tenants shall remain childless or shall not bear children.

DISCRIMINATION BASED ON INCOME

Discrimination on the basis of income is legal. Landlords often require that the prospective tenant have a certain income before the application will be considered.

One test often used is a requirement that the monthly salary be more than four times the monthly rent. The reason for this policy is simple: the landlord is seeking to screen out those people who, because of their inadequate incomes, are likely to default in rent. Unfortunately, any income requirement severely restricts welfare recipients, senior citizens, and other low income persons from finding housing.

If your prospective landlord has an income test, make sure that the joint incomes of both husband and wife are considered by the landlord. In many instances the landlord only considers the income of the husband on the surreptitious reasoning that the wife could become pregnant or lose her job. This would seem to be illegal discrimination against the wife on the basis of sex.

AFFIRMATIVE STEPS TO PROTECT YOURSELF AGAINST DISCRIMINATION

If you have reasonable suspicions that you have been discriminated against, have a friend of different race, creed, color, national origin or sex apply for the apartment. This person used to be called a "straw man" and will be called a "straw person" in this book.

Search for a straw person with financial characteristics substantially similar to you. For example, a good straw person should have an income, profession, length of employment and former residence credentials similar to yours. This confluence of financial credentials and stability help to prove that you were rejected as a tenant solely because of your race, creed, color, national origin, sex or sexual preferences.

FILE A COMPLAINT

You must file a complaint with your local Human Rights Commission or such other state or local agency as may exist in your jurisdiction. You may also file with the Federal Equal Opportunity Commission. You may also be entitled to start a lawsuit. The state or city agency that protects you from discrimination will be found in your local telephone directory under the listing for your state or city. Look for a governmental agency that protects housing, fair practices, human relations and the like.

The Federal, state or city agency will review your case and determine whether your civil rights have been violated. They will bring action against the landlord and see that you get the dwelling.

You may also want to see a private attorney who specializes in these matters. The legislation which protects human rights normally provides for the payment of legal fees to the person discriminated against by the party who has been found guilty of discrimination. The availability of recovering legal fees from the guilty has encouraged many attorneys to practice in this area. For this reason you should have no trouble finding effective representation at affordable cost.

WHOSE NAME SHOULD BE ON THE LEASE?

If you want the absolute right to live in the residence, your name should be on the lease.

HOW TO FIND THE RESIDENCE OF YOUR CHOICE

A whole market is working to provide a residence for you. A market in economic thinking is thousands of people pursuing their own economic best interests or at least what they believe to be their own best economic best interests. And while they pursue their own economic best interests they also pursue your economic best interest by providing goods and services that you want, such as an affordable dwelling of your own.

If you want or need something, chances are there are a number of people out there in the market producing to satisfy your needs. The problem is marrying the buyers with the sellers of the goods.

In this regard, there are providers of services that match sellers with buyers. Those providers of services include classified ads in newspapers, other classified ads, brokers, apartment finding services and roommate placement agencies. Each of these providers of service is briefly discussed below.

But first, try to save time and money by cherry picking the best alternatives through the art of networking.

NETWORKING

Young professionals are good at networking. Learn from them and advertise by word of mouth. Tell all your friends and neighbors that you want an apartment. Tell your relatives, neighborhood merchants, co-workers and acquaintances.

Each person you tell will also have relatives, friends, co-workers neighborhood merchants and acquaintances. Before you know it, you will be hooked into a large network of accumulated knowledge. Any person in the network could know of a person who knows of a residence that may be perfect for you.

A current play on Broadway entitled Six Degrees of Separation by playwright John Guare bears on the importance of networking. The thesis of that play is that only six people separate you from knowing any other person in the world. Think about that. Only six people stand between you and Saddam Hussein. You know your state congressman. He knows President Bush. President Bush knows Secretary of State Baker. And Secretary of State Baker knows Saddam Hussein. In that example only four degrees of separation were necessary.

Lease On Your Terms has been informed that the mathematics of six degrees of separation were developed by a mathematics professor who would defy live audiences to try to invent situations that violated the principal. The professor always won.

The importance of networking is demonstrated by the six degrees of separation. Only six people stand between you and the affordable dwelling of your dreams. The problem lies in finding the right six people.

The moral of the story is that networking always pays and pays large dividends. The reason is that by networking you find information that the rest of the market doesn't yet know. For example, that a friend's uncle has died and an apartment will be available. Or that a friend of a friend is being transferred to a distant state in two months. You are now in a position to exploit that information and convert it to your own advantage.

NEWSPAPER ADS

The real estate section or classified section of your local newspaper is the best place to find out about the market. Read all of the advertisements in order to get a feel for the market in general and the prices for rentals in each neighborhood.

Classified advertisements are written in a kind of short hand code because newspapers charge by the line for each line of print. Most of the abbreviations are self explanatory but the Rosseta Stone of translation to break the most commonly used code is set forth below.

a/c; ac . individual room air conditioner(s)

area . . . as in Central Park area. Really means close to a good address.

bal . . . . balcony

br . . . . bedroom

cen a/c . central air conditioning

cons . . . concessions or inducements for your rental will be given.

dr . . . . Dining Room

dup . . . Duplex on two floors

eik . . . . Eat in kitchen

frpl . . . fireplace

lanai . . . fancy way to say balcony or outside sitting area.

L . . . . . Shaped like the letter "L" with one long room and one short squat room with no wall between them.

lux . . . . Luxury

Pull K . Built in kitchen in which the dining table pulls out of the wall and rests on fold out legs.

riv vu . . River view no matter how slight

so ex . . Southern exposure

wbfp . . Wood burning fireplace

BROKERS

A real estate broker only gets paid if a deal goes through. For a modest commission real estate brokers will teach you about the market. The fee charged by the broker is normally one month's rent or a percentage (from 6% to 10%) of one year's rent. The time of payment of the broker's fee is also negotiable. The fee may be payable at the signing of the lease or in twelve equal monthly installments. It all depends upon the tightness of the market and your relative bargaining position. If you learn nothing else from **Lease On Your Terms**, negotiate, negotiate and negotiate.

A good real estate broker is a treasure of a find like a smart lawyer or a diagnostic doctor. The good broker knows the market, the prices and the neighborhoods. A good broker will save you hours of drudgery in canvassing one dwelling after another looking for something suitable. The broker will not only teach you the market but also correct misapprehensions you may have had as to prices and changing neighborhoods.

You may want to interview and tour with several brokers before you find someone you trust. Tell the broker what you are willing to pay and your requirements for a residence. The broker should be able to winnow out many choices you would only waste your time visiting. Education is normally an expensive commodity. Your broker, however, will teach you a great deal in a short time.

Even if you think you know a city, you will be amazed at how much your broker knows about changing neighborhoods. There is a cyclical nature to the real estate beast. What was a good neighborhood yesterday can become a deteriorating neighborhood today.

There are landlords who list their properties with a broker. This often happens when a private house is listed for sale and winds up leased instead. For this reason it is not always clear who is obligated to pay the broker's commission. If the owner listed the property with the broker, then the owner is responsible for the commission in the first instance. Be careful because the owner will probably try to stick you with the broker's commission or a split of the commission.

Since in theory the real estate broker's commission is paid by the seller, the services of a broker may not cost you one penny. In actuality, the cost of the broker may be a hidden add on to the rent bill.

Lease On Your Terms recommends that you confirm with the broker exactly who is responsible for the broker's fee and the exact amount. **Remember that broker's commission rates and timing of payments are negotiable.** Sometimes they are very negotiable depending on market conditions. Read every piece of paper a broker gives you before you sign it. Actually, reading any legal papers closely before you sign them is a very good idea.

WHEN YOU DO NOT USE A BROKER

If you did not use the services of a broker, you don't want to discover later on that a broker claims to be entitled to be paid.

For this reason **Lease On Your Terms** has a rider that states that you have not utilized the services of a broker and do not expect to pay for the services of any broker in connection with your rental. Use the Tenant's No Broker Clause set forth below and in the FORMS section of this book.

The indemnification language in the clause is the means by which you and the landlord agree to reimburse each other for claims made by a broker. Since you know you did not hire a broker, you are prepared to indemnify the landlord against the broker's commission. You have no way of knowing whether the landlord used a broker. Therefore, you want the landlord to indemnify you against his actions.

The Tenant's No Broker Clause is set forth below and in the FORMS section of this book.

TENANT'S NO BROKER CLAUSE

Landlord and tenant represent, warrant and covenant to each other that no broker brought about this lease. Landlord and tenant each indemnify and hold each other harmless from claims by any broker concerning this lease.

13

WHEN YOU DO USE A BROKER

When either you or the owner do use the services of a broker, it is important to fix (i) the amount of the broker's commission, (ii) the party responsible to pay the commission and (iii) the time or phasing of payment of the commission.

For this reason **Lease On Your Terms** has included a Tenant's Broker Clause set forth below and in the FORMS section of this book.

TENANT'S BROKER CLAUSE

Landlord and tenant represent, warrant and covenant to each other that no broker brought about this lease except for:

_____

Insert name and address of broker

_____.

It is agreed between the parties that the broker's fee will be paid by landlord (tenant).
The amount of the broker's commission is $_____

                                         Insert amount

The broker's commission will be paid at the time and in the manner set forth below:_____

                Insert the time and manner of payment, i.e.

_____

cash or check at signing, in twelve equal payments on the first

_____

day of each month, etc.

_____

_____

_____

_____

_____

PREPARE A BUDGET

How much can you afford each month for rent? How do you know how much you can afford each month for rent? The answer to both of these questions lies in the preparation of a strict budget. Your personal finances are not exactly the national debt of the United States, but on the other hand, you don't have the luxury of raising taxes every time you spend yourself into a deep, depressing deficit.

Rent is a primary expense and must be paid every month in advance of the consumption of the occupancy. You probably don't get paid by your employer until after you render your services. But your rent must still be paid in advance. This can present a cash flow problem to the first time renter.

In order to know where you stand you need a budget. Interesting enough most people do not know where their money goes. They have no idea what they

spend and where they spend it. As a test, carry a pencil and pad around for one month and write down each penny you spend and record what you bought with the money. You will be surprised at the difference between what you think you spend and what you actually spend.

Let's start with your income from all dependable and continuing sources. If your eighty nine year old grandmother sends you $200 each month, you have to make a determination as to whether she is a dependable and continuing source of funds.

You can either prepare your budget on a monthly or weekly basis.

For your convenience the **Lease On Your Terms** Budget Form is set forth below and in the FORMS section of this book.

BUDGET FORM

INCOME

After tax take home salary . . . . _____
Interest income . . . . _____
Dividend income . . . . _____
Alimony . . . . _____
Other . . . . _____
Other . . . . _____
Other . . . . _____
Other . . . . _____

Total . . . . _____

Next let's list your continuing and extraordinary expenses.

EXPENSES

Food . . . . _____
Current rent . . . . _____
Auto notes . . . . _____
Auto operating expense . . . . _____
Commuting to work . . . . _____
Clothes . . . . _____
Entertainment . . . . _____
Miscellaneous . . . . _____
Loan repayments . . . . _____
Alimony . . . . _____
Other . . . . _____
Other . . . . _____
Other . . . . _____
Other . . . . _____
Other . . . . _____

Total . . . . _____

One of Professor Parkinson's Laws is that expenses rise to meet and often exceed income. Don't be shocked if you are spending more than you thought. The trick is to understand where your money is going. Then if you wish, you can save money by shaving unnecessary expenses.

COSTING OUT THE RENT ON THE RESIDENCE

The monthly rent is or may be only one component of the total price each month for the dwelling. It is necessary to ask more questions of the landlord or his agent in order to compute the complete monthly carrying cost of the residence.

You will need to know all the secret charges so that you can see the full cost of the dwelling and insure that it fits into your budget. The Costing Out The Rent Form set forth below and in the FORMS section of this book should ferret out all of the hidden charges.

COSTING OUT THE RENT FORM

Utilities . . . . _____

Electric . . . . _____

Gas . . . . _____

Water . . . . _____

Telephone . . . . _____

Garbage removal . . . . _____

Sewer . . . . _____

Cable TV . . . . _____

Master TV antenna charges . . . . _____

Parking . . . . _____

Laundry . . . . _____

Air Conditioning costs . . . . _____

Amenities (health club, pool, etc.) . . . . _____

Storage space . . . . _____

Other . . . . _____

Other . . . . _____

Other . . . . _____

Other . . . . _____

Total . . . . _____

POPULAR SCAMS

Key Money

The term "key money" relates to money paid in cash in secret for the key to the premises.

The phenomenon known as "key money" occurs in exceptional tight real estate markets like the New York City residential real estate market of the 1980s (before the recession) or like New York City's Chinatown with the present influx of Asian flight money.

The real estate agent listing the residence or the janitor purports to have instructions from the owner to get a downstroke payment equal to six month's rent paid in cash under the table. The reasons are for tax purposes, or to hide the money in a messy divorce or the like. Often there is no receipt and you find that the real estate agent or janitor is a fraud and you are left victimized.

Always verify the identity of the person to whom you are about to pay the money. Get a telephone number, address, bank reference or other secure avenue to track down the person with whom you are dealing.

Legitimate Key Money

There is nothing illegal about key money. In a free market a person is allowed to charge whatever the traffic bears. Key money occurs when the market is so tight that it becomes a virtual seller's market and the sellers are in a position to dictate terms.

Key money is a manner of compensating a tenant who is subletting to you for the cost of improvements made by the tenant to the dwelling. Or for the use of the furnishings left in place for you to use and enjoy.

Always get a receipt for any money you have paid. See the form of receipt below which is reproduced in the forms section of this book.

RECEIPT

RECEIVED ON THE DAY SET FORTH BELOW

FROM_____
          Insert your name

THE SUM OF $_____
          Insert the dollar amount

AS AND FOR A_____.
          Insert the reason for the payment, i.e., down payment,
            advance payment of rent, etc.

THIS MONEY IS (IS NOT) REFUNDABLE UNDER THE FOLLOWING

CONDITIONS:_____
          Insert the conditions concerning a refund

_____

_____

_____

_____
Signature

_____
Title, i.e., manager, agent,
Superintendent, landlord

_____
Street Address

_____
City, State and Zip Code

_____
Telephone number

_____
Form of identification

_____
Insert date

False Advertising

Often the advertisement for residential real estate is not exactly true. More likely the person who runs the advertisement will demand key money (see above) in exchange for getting the residence for you. After you have paid the key money you will find that the person, if still to be found, had no legal entitlement to rent the premises to you and your key money has disappeared.

Bait and Switch Tactics

Often the apartment that appealed to you has just been rented but a more expensive dwelling just happens to be available. These are the ear marks of a bait and switch.

In a bait and switch something low cost or otherwise attractive is offered. The item offered, however, is unavailable when you arrive. But a more expensive alternative is available in abundant supply.

Don't be conned by a bait and switch. If what is offered is unavailable, don't buy the more expensive item. Instead, call your local Consumer Fraud Bureau.

Failure to Return Security Deposits

According to a spokesperson for the Office of the Attorney General of the State of New York, failure to return security deposits is the single most common complaint from tenants about landlords. It is almost as if landlords forget that the security deposit belongs to the tenant. Some landlords appear to think that the security deposit becomes a thirteenth month's rent for each calendar year.

Lease On Your Terms will help protect you from this type of landlord.

The security deposit is your money and does not belong to the landlord. Under the General Obligations Law of the State of New York, your landlord <u>must</u> deposit your security deposit into a separate bank trust account segregated from the landlord's own funds. The landlord must also inform you of the name of the bank. Your landlord cannot co-mingle your security deposit with his own money nor can he spend your deposit. This applies to all tenants regardless of the number of dwellings in the building.

Accordingly, if your landlord goes bankrupt or if his creditors attach his bank account, or if his bank forecloses his mortgage, none of these creditors can touch your trust account.

Even the Internal Revenue Service recognizes that security deposits are not rental income to the landlord. This is one negotiating tool you can use to have your landlord hold your security deposit in trust, if your state law does not already mandate a trust fund concept.

Furthermore, at the end of the lease, you want your landlord to itemize the deductions, if any, he makes from your security deposit.

One state official has told **Lease On Your Terms** that he recommends to tenants that they don't pay the last month's rent when they know that the landlord doesn't return security deposits. The theory is that I would rather have the money when the other guy sues me so that I can be in a position to settle the case on my terms.

Failure to Pay Interest on Security Deposits

A spokesperson for the Office of the Attorney General of one state has told **Lease On Your Terms** that failure to pay interest on security deposits is one of the most common complaints received by his office.

In New York, for example, if your building has six or more apartments, your landlord must add the interest your money earns to your deposit. Furthermore, your landlord must pay all of the accrued interest to you when the deposit is returned to you. The landlord may retain one percent of the interest as an administrative fee.

Miscellaneous Scams

Tricks and tricksters abound. One Judge told **Lease On Your Terms** about a real estate managing agent who was arraigned in his court. The landlord owner of a three hundred plus unit apartment complex advertised "The Jar of Fortune" in which each tenant who signed a lease got to draw a fortune. Winning prizes included two month's free rent and other valuable landlord's concessions.

It turned out that the only winner was the rental agent who filled "The Jar of Fortune" with losing tickets and pocketed over twenty thousand dollars of rental bonuses for himself.

The moral of the story is to explore every gimmick to its logical conclusion. Ask your neighbors who won "Jar of Fortune" or any other such contest.

Roommate Finding Services

Read the fine print in the contract very carefully to be sure of the results you expect for your pre-paid fee. Roommate finding services are probably still unregulated in your jurisdiction.

Classified ads can be expensive. It is probably much cheaper and durable for a qualified owner seeking a qualified roommate to list with a roommate finding service.

Lease On Your Terms believes these services can be well worth the money and will save you a great deal of time. Roommate agencies serve as a clearing house-data bank, listing and sometimes rating available dwellings whose owners seek a roommate. If the listing has been rated and a proper questionnaire matching your preferences with the potential roommate matches, this service could be a blessing.

But the potential for abuse exists. ALWAYS CHECK WITH YOUR LOCAL BETTER BUSINESS BUREAU AND STATE OR LOCAL REGULATORY BODY SUCH AS THE CONSUMER FRAUDS BUREAU OR THE LIKE.

Apartment Finding Services

Alas, **Lease On Your Terms** is saddened to report much abuse exists with apartment finding services. They exist only in such tight markets that dwellings are so unavailable that no one can find an apartment. The paradox, of course, is that if there are no apartments to be found, how can the apartment finding services find any apartments to rent.

Apartment finding services have received a great deal of bad press for valid reasons. They are unregulated by most states and municipalities. They charge a non-returnable fee in advance of the service being rendered. Often they render no service except to furnish a rehash of the local classified sections from old issues of the local newspapers.

Lease On Your Terms advises that you consult with your local Better Business Bureau and state or local regulatory agency such as the Consumer Frauds Bureau prior to passing any money to an apartment finding service. Alternatively, pay only after the apartment finding service has found you a suitable apartment and you have a signed lease for the premises.

PART 2

PROBLEMS OF INSPECTING THE PREMISES

VIEWING THE PROPERTY

You will want to view the property before you sign a lease to rent it.

Ask the landlord or his agent whether you can see a floor plan of the dwelling. Check the overall layout of the residence and the size of the rooms. Remember that you are measuring in your mind's eye from interior wall to interior wall. The landlord's floor plan measures from outside wall to outside wall for his floor plan measurements. That's the reason why each room will appear smaller than it should to be based upon the floor plan.

Bring a tape measure with you. Measure the width of the doorways and walls to verify that your furniture will fit into each room.

Sometimes it is inconvenient for the landlord or his agent to visit the premises with you. In that case the Property Viewing and Keys Agreement set forth below and in the FORMS section of this book solves the problem by allowing the landlord to trust you with the keys.

PROPERTY VIEWING AND KEYS AGREEMENT

I hereby acknowledge receipt of the key(s) to the dwelling at

_____.

I shall use the key(s) for the express purpose of viewing the dwelling in order to determine whether it is suitable for rental by me.

I have given the landlord or his agent a key deposit of $_____ receipt of which is hereby acknowledged. The key deposit shall be returned to me when I return the key(s).

I shall return the key(s) by_____(a.m.) (p.m.) today to the landlord or his agent at the same place where I received the key(s). Should I fail to return the key(s), the landlord is entitled to retain my deposit to pay for the cost of changing the locks on the dwelling.

_____

Insert your name Prospective Tenant

_____

Insert your street address

_____

Insert your city, state and zip code

_____

Insert your telephone reach number

_____

Insert date

RECEIPT OF ABOVE DEPOSIT ACKNOWLEDGED

_____

Landlord or agent.

RECORD OF VIEWING OF PREMISES

You will probably look at more than one potential residence before you have made a final selection. After a while each of the premises you have seen will begin to merge in your mind. You will forget which dwelling had the free health club, which the river view and the rent on yet another.

The following checklist will serve as a record of each of the premises you have seen. It is designed to refresh your memory regarding the salient features of each of the dwellings and the costs.

Lease On Your Terms recommends that you fill out a Record of Viewing for each dwelling during your

visit while all of the facts are at your disposal and fresh in your mind. Later on when your mind turns to fudge you will have all of the reliable data you need to refresh your recollection in one place. This is what trial lawyers call past recollection refreshed.

Lease On Your Terms also recommends that you rate each dwelling in order of acceptable priority to you. Keep updating your preference list as you view more prospective dwellings.

The **Lease On Your Terms** Record of Viewing of Premises is set forth below. For your convenience several copies are reprinted in the FORMS section at the end of this book.

RECORD OF VIEWING CHECKLIST

ADDRESS _____
_____
_____

TYPE OF BUILDING_____
(garden apartment, brownstone, hi-rise, home, luxury, loft, etc.)

NUMBER OF ROOMS _____

TYPE OF ROOMS_____
_____
_____
_____

MONTHLY RENT $_____

NUMBER OF MONTH'S ADVANCE RENT _____

SECURITY DEPOSIT $_____

TYPE OF KITCHEN_____

AIR CONDITIONING_____

APPLIANCES_____

SQUARE FEET OF LIVING SPACE_____
PARKING_____

ESTIMATED COST OF UTILITIES_____
_____

AMENITIES_____
_____
_____
_____

SECURITY & DOORMAN_____

LAUNDRY_____

PROXIMITY TO SHOPPING_____
_____
_____

SCHOOL DISTRICT_____

COMMUTE TO WORK_____
_____
_____

CABLE TV_____

STORAGE BINS_____

TOTAL COST PER MONTH:
Rent . . . . _____
Utilities . . . . _____
Parking . . . . _____
Cable TV . . . . _____
Amenities . . . . _____
Laundry . . . . _____
Storage bins . . . . _____
Other . . . . _____
Other . . . . _____
Other . . . . _____
Other . . . . _____
Other . . . . _____
Other . . . . _____

TOTAL COST . . . . ._____

WHAT DID YOU LIKE ABOUT THIS AS A RESIDENCE?

_____
_____
_____
_____
_____
_____
_____
_____
_____
_____

WHAT DID YOU DISLIKE ABOUT THIS AS A RESIDENCE?

_____
_____
_____
_____
_____
_____
_____
_____
_____
_____

OVER-ALL RATING_____

HOW TO PROTECT YOURSELF AGAINST PUFFING

Any seller of goods, including a landlord, is allowed to "Puff up" the quality of his goods. Puffing is defined as loose, general, commendatory sales talk concerning the inherent value and quality of goods for sale. Puffing is legal. Outright lying, on the other hand is illegal fraud.

The fine line between puffing and fraud depends upon (i) how substantial is the inducement and (ii) whether the mental intent of the landlord was to deceive.

There are two types of fraud. There is fraud by commission and fraud by omission. Fraud by commission involves the use of a false or deceptive promise. Thus, deception, false pretense, false promise, and misrepresentation are all forms of fraud.

Fraud by omission involves the failure to tell you or the concealment of something material. Knowing concealment, suppression or omission of any material fact with the intent that others rely upon such concealment, suppression or omission are also the indices of fraud.

In one classic case, for example, the court found fraud where a promised swimming pool facility and play area were not provided by the owner.

Most sellers puff their goods and services. Your car dealer is always comparing the cheapest imported car to a BMW or Porsche, when he really knows from complaints at the service department that the car is like an orange crate on wheels. In order to discover the truth, you check with **Consumer Reports** and other independent testing agencies, test drive the car and ask other owners about their satisfaction level with the automobile and the dealer.

Do the same testing with the dwelling. If you ask the landlord whether this is a quiet neighborhood, what do you think he will say? Verify his answer by visiting the apartment during rush hour, at night, on weekends and during the day at various times in order to determine for yourself how quiet the apartment actually is. Also ask the neighbors.

If any fact about the apartment is important to you, verify this fact by means independent of the landlord.

LANDLORD'S ORAL REPRESENTATIONS ARE UNENFORCEABLE

A standard clause in most leases states that the lease constitutes the full agreement between the parties and that there have been no oral representations made by the landlord or his agent.

This clause is called the "shut off" clause. Its purpose is to shut off any oral representations or inducements made by the landlord or his agent in order to entice you into signing the lease. Beware of this clause and take care to write into the lease any oral statements that you believe has been promised to you.

On occasion oral representations are made. Or more likely there are misunderstandings. The landlord or his agent may have made casual statements. You may have been misinformed by loose conversation during the sales pitch. You may have interpreted the landlord's statement as a binding commitment.

There is rule of evidence which prohibits the admission of oral testimony to contradict, alter or vary the terms of a written document which is complete on its face. Lawyers call this the parole evidence rule.

In sum, a lease provision that there have been no representations or understandings other than those contained in the lease is legitimate. Where substantial representations were made and not honored, there is an effective remedy available. But you don't want an effective legal remedy that forces you to go to court for enforcement **after you have proved your case.** You want any oral promises written into the TENANT'S ORAL REPRESENTATION CLAUSE.

You want to prevent the landlord or his agent from misrepresenting any aspects of the deal to you. The word misrepresent is a fancy word for deceive and lie by commission or omission. In other words deceit by covering up important facts or by omitting to tell the truth. **Use the Tenant's oral representation clause to document any important oral representations made to you or understood by you to be part of the deal. If it's not in writing, it's not in the lease.**

All you have to do is list any oral promises by the landlord or his agent in the Tenant's Oral Representation Clause set forth below and in the FORMS section of this book.

TENANT'S ORAL REPRESENTATION CLAUSE

This lease constitutes the full agreement between the parties and there have been no oral representations made except for the following oral representations made by the landlord:

1. Insert landlord's oral representations

2.

3.

4.

HOW THE LANDLORD PROTECTS AGAINST YOUR PUFFING

Just as the landlord is allowed to puff the quality of his dwelling, you are allowed to puff up your qualities as a prospective tenant. Just as you are checking and verifying everything important about the dwelling to you such as the noise level, the proximity to shopping, the landlord's policy on lease renewals and return of security deposits and the like, the landlord wants to check up on you.

The landlord wants to qualify you as the type of caring, peaceful, and financially responsible tenant he really wants. Probably from the landlord's point of view a traveling salesman who is never home is the best kind of tenant, because that tenant makes no demands on the landlord's infrastructure.

The landlord wants to verify and is entitled to verify your credit standing in the community. Under the Federal Fair Credit Reporting Act your landlord can obtain a copy of your Consumer Report from a Consumer Reporting Agency also known as in the trade as a credit bureau. Your landlord has a definite business purpose related to a lease which is a business transaction involving you. Your Consumer Report is compiled by the credit bureaus to lubricate the wheels of commerce. For further information on the subject of Your Consumer Report see the book **How to Erase Bad Credit** by the author of this book.

Don't be afraid if the landlord tells you that he intends to draw or request a credit report on your credit standing. He has a right to do so and is legally entitled to get a copy of your Consumer Report with or without your consent. The landlord may also ask you to pay his cost of obtaining your credit report. This is a matter of negotiation. Once again you are in a negotiation zone. You can tell the landlord that this is his expense of doing business, especially since he is such a bad judge of character that he refuses to take your assurance on this matter.

Whether or not you pay for the credit check depends upon your relative bargaining power. Also you could ask for the credit fee to be returned if the landlord approves you as tenant or selects another tenant prior to checking your credit history.

The cost of a Consumer Report varies from state to state. Normally landlords belong to trade associations that are subscribing members of Consumer Reporting Agencies. The trade associations obtain Consumer Reports at discounted bulk rates. The cost of a copy of your Consumer Report should run between eight and fifty dollars depending on where you live.

A Credit Verification Agreement Form is set forth below and in the FORMS section of this book. The only reason to use this Form is as a receipt for the fee charged by the landlord and to record your agreement with the landlord regarding the conditions under which the fee will be returned to you.

CREDIT VERIFICATION AND REFUND AGREEMENT FORM

RECEIVED FROM_____
Insert your name

as a prospective tenant the sum of $_____

to be used solely for the purpose of requesting a Consumer Report under the Federal Fair Credit Reporting Act and otherwise verifying the information submitted on an application to rent premises situate at and commonly known as_____
Insert street, city and state address

_____.

This sum is to be refunded if (i) the landlord or his agent ("landlord") selects another tenant to rent the dwelling prior to requesting the Consumer Report or (ii) a lease is signed between landlord and this prospective tenant.

_____
Landlord or agent

_____
Prospective tenant

_____
Date

_____
Time

THE RENTAL APPLICATION

The landlord will also want you to sign his form of rental application. The rental application looks like an intimidating invasion of your privacy. It will look worse than the forms you fill out for a top secret security clearance from the United States Department of Defense. It will look like every employment application you have ever filled out. We all know what happens if you fail to fill out an employment application. Chances are you will not get the job. The employer will assume that you have too much to hide.

No one knows what happens if you fail to fill out the rental application. Or if you lie in any material respect. Most of the information the landlord wants to know is easily verifiable from your Consumer Report which is maintained by Consumer Reporting Agencies under the Federal Fair Credit Reporting Act.

Furthermore, a conscientious landlord wants to obtain the best qualified tenant to safeguard the value of the his property. That kind of landlord will want to dig out all the facts. To some degree applying for a rental dwelling is like applying for a job. Other than your general knowledge of market conditions, you have no idea how many other applicants are being considered by the landlord.

Lease On Your Terms recommends basic honesty in filling out the rental application. We recommend honesty not because it is the best policy but because honesty generally works. While honesty is a relative concept, we don't recommend stupid lies that are easily discovered. If something in your background worries you, tell the landlord and explain it away before the landlord wrongly assumes the worst.

The rental application will seek information that appears to be prying into your personal life. It will appear that the only purpose for needing the information is to allow the landlord to track you or your money down, if you breach the lease. For example, the landlord will want to know whom to contact in an emergency. At first blush this looks a hook to track you down when you break the lease and cut and run. But what if you are murdered or die of natural causes in the dwelling? Suppose you need emergency surgery and the next of kin has to be notified?

Lease On Your Terms advises that you should not enter a commercial transaction with the thought of how do I cut and run when I default. We do suggest that you do analyze each question on the rental application with a jaundiced eye. Remember that all appears yellow to a jaundiced eye. Accordingly, ask the landlord why he needs information that appears questionable or peripheral to you. If no reasonable and satisfactory answer is given to you, you may say so and civilly decline to answer that question at this time.

The rental application may ask for the following types of information:

1. Identification, i.e. driver's license number.

2. Social Security number. The landlord needs your Social Security number in order to draw your Consumer Report from a Consumer Reporting Agency under the Federal Fair Credit Reporting Act. Your Social Security number separates you from all the other people in the data base that have names the same or similar to yours.

3. Date of Birth. Same story as your Social Security number. DOB is needed to identify you from all the other people with the same name in the credit bureau records.

4. Employment verification.

5. Salary

6. Previous addresses.

7. Previous landlord's names and addresses.

8. Relationships of those who will live with you.

9. Bank references and account numbers.

10. Make of auto

11. Personal references

12. Credit references

REQUEST FOR VERIFICATION OF BANK DEPOSIT

A careful landlord may also wish to verify the deposit balances in your bank accounts. This is also a touchy area in which you may believe that your privacy is being violated. The landlord merely wants to verify that you have the financial cushion necessary to meet his rent payments during your times of adversity. You may think your landlord is trying to find where your assets are so that he can levy on them after he sues you. This is possible but far fetched. You can change bank accounts faster than your landlord can find them.

Your landlord may or may not need you to sign a form authorizing your bank to release information about your accounts. This will depend upon your local law and official bank policy.

He could probably get his banker to do a bank to bank inquiry and get rough information furnished over the counter to the trade such as "maintains balances in the low five figures".

In any event, don't panic. Unless you call your bank and tell them not to release information, the chances are that the inter-bank grapevine will operate.

DEPOSITS

We are now talking about a deposit submitted to the landlord at the same time that the tenant executes and delivers the rental application. It is the experience of **Lease On Your Terms** that landlords prefer to receive "up front" rental deposits.

The reasons are psychological as well as financial. Landlords feel that a tenant who has left a deposit to hold a dwelling is psychologically committed to rent from them. Landlords also want to weed out the totally frivolous tenant by holding a good faith deposit.

Lease On Your Terms advises that deposits are a matter of negotiation. If you are in a tight rental market with few available dwellings, then you want to leave a deposit provided that the landlord takes the unit off the market or otherwise reserves the unit for you. If you are in a buyer's market with a lot of available housing, then the deposit only ties you up with no benefit to you.

If you do leave a deposit you will need a receipt for the deposit and a deposit agreement stating the exact nature of your agreement with the landlord. **Lease On Your Terms** has provided a Tenant's Deposit Agreement Form set forth below and in the FORMS section of this book.

TENANT'S DEPOSIT AGREEMENT FORM

Landlord hereby acknowledges receipt of the sum of $_____

Insert amount of deposit

received from _____

          Insert name of tenant(s)

(hereinafter referred to as the "prospective tenant(s)") to be held by landlord as a totally refundable deposit for the purpose of holding premises situate and known as (Insert unit number, street, city and state address and zip code):

_____

_____

_____

until _____

          Insert date when reservation of unit terminates

or until the landlord verifies prospective tenant(s)' rental application.

    This deposit shall be totally refundable to the prospective tenant(s) whether or not the prospective tenant shall rent the premises.

_____

Landlord

_____

Prospective Tenant(s)

_____

Prospective Tenant(s)

_____

Date

THE LANDLORD'S SELECTION PROCESS

The landlord will select the best possible tenant based upon the information each tenant has furnished to the landlord. This is one of the reasons that you want to be as candid as possible in the rental application. Since the landlord is making a decision based on information given by you, it should be easy for you to stack the deck of information in your favor. Explain away any rough edges before they can embarrass you.

The actual selection process will vary from landlord to landlord but is not unlike the job selection process. Landlords cannot discriminate illegally in renting any more than employers can in hiring practices. Each interviews as many possible candidates for the opening until the best possible person suited within the time available to fill the vacancy appears. Landlords have no more obligation to rent to the person with the earliest dated rental application than employers have to hire the first person interviewed for a job.

YOU TAKE THE PREMISES "AS IS"

Under most forms of residential lease you take the rented premises "as is" and have a responsibility to re-deliver the premises to the landlord without damage to it, except for damage which occurs through ordinary wear and tear.

The term "as is" means just that. Problems may occur at the end of the lease. When you surrender the premises to the landlord, how do you prove the original condition upon your acceptance of the premises? Remember the landlord is trying to hold you liable for any damage and has your security deposit. **The answer is to use the checklists set forth in the Tenant's Guide and to detail every scratch, chip, dent and imperfection on the list which you and the landlord will sign.**

REASONABLE WEAR AND TEAR EXCEPTED

Most things have a definable useful life. A pair of sneakers, a pair of shoes, a sink, a refrigerator and every other tangible physical thing will age and deteriorate with the passage of time. Reasonable wear and tear is the damage done by ordinary usage and the passage of time. Just envision the door mat of your house or car and its decay over time. You should assume that your responsibility under the lease is generally to take good care of the rented premises and all of the landlord' property attached to those premises.

Many landlords equate the phrases "to let" and "toilet". Try to use the same standard of care in protecting the landlord's property as you use in protecting your own property and you should never have any problems.

The way you prove ordinary wear and tear to the landlord at the end of the lease is to compare the present state of the premises with the detailed checklists set forth in the Tenant's Guide. Those checklists should be signed by you and the landlord on the day you originally inspected the premises. Don't hesitate to minutely note each imperfection on your inspection list because landlord's are shameless at the end of the lease in finding untoward damage to their beloved apartments.

TAKE PICTURES

Don't forget to take pictures of any pre-existing damage to the residence. A picture is worth a thousand witnesses in a dispute over alleged damage to the premises if, as and when the landlord sues for damages or you want your security deposit returned.

In these days of instant cameras, camcorders and polaroid pictures you can get same day satisfactory pictures in the flash of a camera.

Lease On Your Terms has never met a landlord who did not think his property was the Taj Mahal or at least worth more than Boardwalk and Park Place combined.

USE THE DETAILED CHECKLISTS

The checklists printed below will provide evidence of the condition of the residence prior to the time possession was given to you by the landlord. Preferably you and the landlord or the landlord's agent should examine the premises together. You should both participate in the preparation of the checklist and should both sign the checklists. If the landlord refuses to sign the checklist get an impartial witness to examine the premises with you.

It is serviceable to describe counter tops, sinks, bath tubs, refrigerators, and the like as "dented, scratched, chipped soiled, stained, and peeling". Greater specificity is not needed.

The checklist should also be dated.

HOW TO QUALIFY A WRITING AS A BUSINESS RECORD

A writing is hearsay and cannot be introduced into evidence at a trial or hearing unless it is qualified as a business record. Here's how to make sure that your checklist is a business record.

A business record has to have been maintained in accordance with a business transaction, has to made simultaneous with the transactions recorded in the record, and has to accurately reflect the matters set forth in the business record. It also has to be your practice to keep such records.

In this case, the business is the business of the lease transaction. The checklist meets all of the above criteria. It should become a business record made in the ordinary course of business. The consequences are that business records are admissible in evidence should you and the landlord fight over your security deposit return or alleged damages to the premises.

In order to introduce the checklist into evidence you will have to authenticate the checklist by saying the words in the above paragraph.

If the judge refuses to admit the checklist as a business record, it still is good as an admission against the landlord's interest if signed by the landlord.

The checklist is also admissible to refresh your recollection of the exact condition of the premises.

Use the checklists. The checklists are to landlords what silver bullets are to werewolves.

REMEMBER TO CHANGE THE LOCKS TO THE DWELLING WHEN YOU MOVE IN. YOU NORMALLY DON'T HAVE TO REPLACE THE ENTIRE LOCK; CHANGING THE TUMBLERS IS MUCH CHEAPER.

CHECK LIST

PREMISES SITUATE AT

_____

_____

_____

This checklist was made by the tenant(s) prior to moving into the above stated premises. All notes reflected in this checklist were made contemporaneously with the an examination of the premises by the tenant(s) and the landlord or witness.

This checklist is made to serve as a business record of the events recorded herein, namely the condition of the premises prior to the date the tenant(s) took possession of the premises.

The landlord or his agent have been invited to join in the preparation of this check list and have (have not) participated.

_____
Tenant(s)

_____
Witness

_____
Landlord

_____
Date

CHECK LIST

ENTRY ROOM

Ceiling and Walls—describe any holes. State size and depth in inches or millimeters.

_____

_____

Describe any cracks and the length of each._____

_____

_____

Falling plaster_____

_____

Peeling paint_____

_____

Look for discolored yellow or brown marks indicating water leaks
from the floor above and describe them._____

_____

_____

_____

Floor—describe any holes and the size and depth of each in inches or
millimeters._____

_____

_____

Note any soft spots where floor gives when stepped on.

_____

_____

Note any significant degree of slant._____

_____

Note any ripped or cracked linoleum or floor covering._____

_____

_____

Windows—Inspect glass closely.
Note any cracks, holes, or missing glass._____

_____

_____

Check window panes for loose putty and note if panes are loose in the
mullions._____

_____

_____

Open windows and note if they slide up and down._____

_____
_____
_____

Note whether windows stay in raised position without falling.

_____
_____
_____

Inspect screens and storms for serviceability and note rips, cracks and tears etc._____

_____
_____
_____

Note whether there is a lock on the window and does it work?_____

_____
_____
_____

Is there a fire escape and how secure is it for escape and to keep out intruders?_____

_____
_____
_____

Check windows for drafts._____

_____
_____

Electrical—Count the number of electrical outlets. Verify and note whether they work._____

_____
_____

Do all light switches work?_____

_____
_____

Is there unwrapped and exposed wiring in contravention of building codes? If so, note where._____

_____
_____

Check fuse box and note the amperage and voltage._____

_____
_____
_____

Do fuses blow? often?_____

_____

Heat

Is there sufficient heat?_____

_____
_____

Check radiators and note if the entire radiator heats up._____

_____
_____

Check radiators and note whether there are turn off handles.

_____
_____

Note if the turn handles are broken, missing or locked so that the radiator
cannot be turned on and off._____

_____
_____

Note whether the radiator leaks._____

_____
_____

DOORS

Note whether the doors close properly and securely._____

_____
_____
_____
_____
_____
_____

Check the locks. Note if each entrance has at least one dead bolt secure lock.
(A dead bold lock cannot be picked and forces thieves who otherwise gain entrance
to the apartment to carry your personal goods out of a window which thieves don't relish
for obvious reasons.)_____

_____
_____
_____

Check and note any damage to the surfaces on both sides of each
door._____

_____
_____
_____
_____
_____

Note if there too much space on the top, bottom or sides of any door which render the door insecure._____

_____
_____
_____
_____

Operate the door handles and note if they work and to insure that no parts are missing._____

_____
_____
_____
_____

Front Door
Note if there a peep hole for security._____

_____

Note whether there is a Fox police lock or other reinforced bar bolting the door into a plate on the floor.

KITCHEN CHECKLIST

Plumbing
Note any leaks in and under pipes and faucets._____

_____
_____
_____
_____

Note any broken handles on sinks._____

_____
_____
_____
_____

Note any chipped and pitted porcelain on sinks._____

_____
_____
_____
_____

Note whether faucets run or drip or leak._____

_____
_____
_____
_____

Is there sufficient hot water in the kitchen sink?_____

_____
_____
_____

Sink

Is there adequate water pressure?_____

_____

Is there sufficient hot and cold water?_____

_____

Is the water clean and drinkable?_____

_____
_____

Note any leaks under the drain._____

_____
_____
_____

Does water drain from the sink without problems?_____

_____

Note if the faucets are dripping, need washers or show that other visible plumbing problems
exist._____

_____
_____

Note if the drains are stopped, stuffed or slow in draining
water._____

_____
_____

Note if the faucets have handles and spigots that work._____

_____
_____

Check porcelain in sinks and note chips, pits, dents, discoloration and other unsightly
scratches that the landlord may try to charge to your security deposit._____

_____
_____
_____
_____

Appliances

Refrigerator

Note any scratches, chips, pits, dents, discoloration or other damage to the inside or outside of the refrigerator which the landlord may try to charge to your security deposit._____

_____

_____

_____

_____

Note any missing handles, knobs, shelves, trays or doors._____

_____

_____

_____

_____

Check the inside temperature and note whether the refrigerator works and that the freezer will keep food frozen without needing the highest setting._____

_____

_____

_____

_____

Note the BTU usage in order to determine how energy efficient the refrigerator is._____

_____

_____

Check door gaskets and note if the insulation is sufficient or if the gaskets need to be changed._____

_____

_____

_____

Note if the gaskets fit properly and whether they are in good condition._____

_____

___ _____

_____

Count and note the ice cube trays and their condition._____

_____

_____

_____

Verify and note whether all convenience items (automatic defroster, automatic ice maker and the like) are in good working order._____

_____

_____

_____

_____

Stove

Turn on each of the burners. Note whether each of the burners work._____
_____
_____
_____

Note whether the oven works._____
_____
_____

Check the inside of the oven for cleanliness, chips, dents, abrasions
 discoloration etc. and note the condition.
_____
_____
_____
_____
_____
_____

Note any damage to the inside and outside of the oven caused by cracks, dents
 chips or scratches to the porcelain. Note any stains on the inside of the oven._____
_____
_____
_____
_____

Note any missing or broken handles or parts to the stove.
_____
_____
_____
_____

Verify and note whether all convenience gimmicks like the clock,
timer, etc are in good working condition._____
_____
_____
_____
_____
_____

Insects

Look for and note evidence of infestation of roaches, mice, rats and other
undesirables._____
_____
_____
_____
_____

Note any mouse holes or similar holes in the walls, especially common walls into neighboring apartments._____

_____
_____
_____
_____
_____

Obtain the name of the exterminator used by the landlord. This will usually be the cheapest and most reliable exterminator you will be able to find. Verify and note who is responsible for extermination._____

_____
_____
_____
_____

Note how often the exterminator is scheduled to come, what areas does he spray and what pesticides does he use, because it may be hazardous to your family or your pets.

_____
_____
_____
_____
_____

Cabinets
Note any damage to the kitchen cabinets._____

_____
_____
_____
_____
_____

Note any scratches, dents, discolorations, bad or peeling paint jobs and missing handles or shelves._____

_____
_____
_____
_____
_____

Note the condition of the hinges and whether the hinges are affixed solidly._____

_____
_____
_____

Note whether there sufficient cabinet space for you or will you have to add more at your expense or at the landlord's expense.

_____
_____

BATHROOM CHECKLIST

Sink

Note whether there is adequate water pressure in all water taps in the sinks, bathtub and shower._____

_____

_____

_____

Note whether there sufficient hot and cold water in all water taps in the sinks, bathtub and shower._____

_____

_____

_____

Note whether the water from each tap is clean and drinkable?

_____

_____

_____

_____

Check for and note leaks under the drain._____

_____

_____

Note whether the water drains from sinks and tubs without problems._____

_____

_____

_____

_____

Note whether the faucets drip, need washers or whether other visible plumbing problems exist.

_____

_____

_____

_____

Note whether the drains are stopped, stuffed or slow in draining water._____

_____

_____

_____

Note whether the faucets have handles and spigots that work.

_____

_____

_____

_____

Check porcelain in sinks and tub; note chips, pits, dents, discoloration and other unsightly scratches that the landlord may try to charge to your security deposit.

_____
_____
_____
_____
_____
_____
_____

Cabinets

Note whether the bathroom cabinets are damaged._____

_____
_____
_____
_____
_____

Note any scratches, dents, discolorations, bad or peeling paint jobs and missing handles or shelves._____

_____
_____
_____
_____
_____
_____
_____
_____

Note whether there sufficient cabinet space for you or whether you have to add more at your expense._____

_____
_____
_____
_____

Bath Tub

Note whether there is adequate water pressure in all taps.

_____
_____
_____
_____

Note whether there sufficient hot and cold water in all taps.

_____
_____
_____
_____

Note whether the water from all taps is clean and drinkable.

_____
_____
_____
_____

Note whether there are any leaks._____
_____
_____

Note whether water drains from the tub without problems_____
_____

Note whether the faucets drip, need washers or whether other visible plumbing problems
exist._____
_____
_____
_____
_____

Note whether the drain is stopped, stuffed or slow in draining
water._____
_____
_____

Note whether the faucets have handles and spigots that work.
_____
_____
_____

Check the porcelain in the tub and note chips, pits, dents, discoloration and
other unsightly scratches that the landlord may try to charge to your security deposit
_____
_____
_____
_____
_____

Mirror

Note whether the mirror over the sink is broken, cracked or discolored._____
_____
_____
_____
_____

Note whether the mirror is blotchy and needs resilvering in
places._____
_____
_____
_____

Note whether there a medicine cabinet and if the hinges work and their condition.

_____
_____
_____
_____
_____
_____

Examine the medicine cabinet shelves and note rust stains, discoloration and
other evidence of damage._____
_____
_____
_____
_____

Tiles

Note whether there missing, loose, cracked or unmatching bathroom tiles.

_____
_____
_____
_____
_____

Examine the grout and note mildew or evidence that new grout is
necessary to hold the tiles in place._____
_____
_____
_____
_____

Commodes

Note any broken handles on commodes._____
_____
_____
_____

Note any chipped and pitted porcelain on commodes._____
_____
_____
_____

Note whether toilet runs, drips or leaks._____
_____
_____

Note whether toilet flushes completely after each flush._____
_____

Note whether toilet seat is securely attached._____

_____

_____

Note whether toilet seat is broken, chipped or cracked?_____

_____

LIVING ROOM CHECK LIST

LIVING ROOM
Ceiling and Walls—describe any holes. State size and depth in inches or millimeters.

_____

_____

Describe any cracks and the length of each.

_____

_____

_____

_____

Falling plaster.

_____

_____

Peeling paint

_____

_____

Look for discolored yellow or brown marks indicating water leaks form the
floor above and describe them.

_____

_____

_____

Floor—describe any holes and the size and depth of each in inches or millimeters.

_____

_____

_____

Note any soft spots where floor gives when stepped on.

_____

_____

_____

Note any significant degree of slant.

_____

_____

Note any ripped or cracked linoleum or the condition of other floor covering such as carpeting or rugs._____

_____
_____
_____

Windows—Inspect glass closely.
Note any cracks, holes, or missing glass._____

_____
_____
_____

Check window panes for loose putty and note if panes are loose in the mullions._____

_____
_____
_____
_____

Open windows and note if they slide up and down._____

_____
_____
_____

Note whether windows stay in raised position without falling.

_____
_____
_____

Inspect screens and storms for serviceability and note rips, cracks and tears etc.

_____
_____
_____

Note whether there a lock on the window and does it work?_____

_____
_____
_____

Is there a fire escape and how secure is it for escape and to keep out intruders?_____

_____
_____

Check windows for drafts._____

_____

Electrical—Count the number of electrical outlets. Verify and note whether they work._____

_____
_____

Do all light switches work?_____

Is there unwrapped and exposed wiring in contravention of building codes? If so, note where._____

_____
_____

Heat

Is there sufficient heat?_____

_____
_____

Check radiators and note if the entire radiator heats up._____

_____
_____

Check radiators and note whether there are turn off handles.

_____
_____

Note if the turn handles broken, missing or locked so that the radiator cannot be turned on and off._____

_____
_____

Note whether the radiator leaks._____

_____
_____

Telephone Jacks

Note whether there enough telephone Jacks in conveniently located places._____

_____
_____
_____
_____

BEDROOM CHECK LIST

BED ROOM

Ceiling and Walls—describe any holes. State size and depth in inches or millimeters._____

_____

Describe any cracks and the length of each._____

_____
_____
_____

Falling plaster_____

_____

Peeling paint_____

_____

Look for discolored yellow or brown marks indicating water leaks form the floor above and describe them._____

_____
_____

Floor—describe any holes and the size and depth of each in inches or millimeters._____

_____
_____

Note any soft spots where floor gives when stepped on._____

_____
_____

Note any significant degree of slant._____

_____
_____

Note any ripped or cracked linoleum or the condition of other floor covering such as carpeting or rugs._____

_____
_____

Windows—Inspect glass closely.

Note any cracks, holes, or missing glass._____
_____
_____
_____

Check window panes for loose putty and note if panes are loose in the
mullions._____
_____
_____
_____
_____

Open windows and note if they slide up and down._____
_____
_____
_____

Note whether windows stay in raised position without falling.
_____
_____
_____

Inspect screens and storms for serviceability and note rips, cracks and tears etc.
_____
_____
_____

Note whether there is a lock on the window and does it work?
_____
_____
_____

Is there a fire escape and how secure is it for escape and to keep out intruders?
_____
_____
_____

Check windows for drafts._____
_____
_____

Electrical—Count the number of electrical outlets. Verify and note whether they work.
_____
_____
_____

Do all light switches work?_____
_____
_____

Is there unwrapped and exposed wiring in contravention of building codes? If so,

note where._____
_____
_____

Heat

Is there sufficient heat?_____
_____
_____

Check radiators and note if the entire radiator heats up._____
_____
_____

Check radiators and note whether there are turn off handles.
_____
_____

Note if the turn handles broken, missing or locked so that the radiator
cannot be turned on and off._____
_____
_____

Note whether the radiator leaks._____
_____
_____

Telephone Jacks

Note whether there enough telephone Jacks in conveniently located places.
_____
_____
_____
_____
_____

MISCELLANEOUS

Verify that the Heat and Air Conditioning in each room is suitable to your
needs and note any deficiencies in their operating systems or housings.

_____
_____
_____
_____
_____
_____
_____
_____
_____

Note whether all telephone jacks in the residence are working.

_____
_____
_____

Note whether there are trash bins and the days of rubbish removal. Also note
whether refuse must be recycled. Note who removes trash and the cost to you, if any.

_____
_____
_____
_____
_____
_____

Note the condition of the closet space including whether the
bars for hanging clothes are securely affixed to the wall on each side.

_____
_____
_____
_____
_____

Note whether there is a storage bin in the basement that comes with the dwelling.
Note the cost to you, if any. Note the condition of the bin and any apparent damage
to the bin._____
_____
_____
_____
_____

Determine and note whether utilities are included in the rent or
must you pay the electric, gas and water bill directly to the utility.

_____
_____
_____
_____
_____
_____

Get estimates as to the monthly cost of each of the utilities and note the estimated cost of each._____

_____

_____

_____

_____

_____

_____

Note whether there separate gas, electric and water meters for each apartment.
If not, verify and note how the landlord apportions the bills.

_____

_____

_____

_____

_____

Check the overall layout of the floor plan of the residence.
Note the size of each room from the floor plan in width and length.

_____

_____

_____

_____

_____

Try to get a fix on the amount of noise audible in the dwelling from outside sources.
Open the windows and note the noise level.
Note the condition of carpets which insulate the noise._____

_____

_____

_____

_____

Is there a laundry on the premises?   Is it run by the landlord or the tenants?
Note the cost, the hours of operation and the arrangements.

_____

_____

_____

_____

Note whether there a parking lot in the building and a space allocated for your car.
Note the monthly charges. Note where guests park. What if you are a two car family?

_____

_____

_____

_____

_____

Note whether there is a master antenna on the roof with which you can hook up.
Note whether the building is wired for cable TV and the cost of any hook-ups.

_____
_____
_____

Note whether the building has a health club, swimming pool, sauna or other amenities.
Note the fee or charge to use the facilities.

_____
_____
_____
_____
_____

Note whether there is a doorman and note his duties. _____
Note the special services the door man provides and the hours he is in attendance.

_____
_____
_____
_____

Note the security arrangements surrounding the dwelling.
Note whether each residence has a peep hole viewer in the front door, a smoke alarm,
fire extinguisher, chain lock on the front door, dead bolt locks, Fox floor to door police
locks and reliable guards._____

_____
_____
_____
_____
_____
_____

Note whether each room has a radiator or heat vent._____

_____
_____
_____
_____

Note whether each room has an air conditioner or vent._____

_____
_____
_____
_____
_____

A REMINDER

Don't forget to take pictures of any pre-existing damage to the residence.

PART 3

NEGOTIATING FOR YOUR CHANGES TO THE LANDLORD'S FORM OF THE LEASE

THE ART OF NEGOTIATION

Everything in the world has a price and every price is negotiable.

A classic story on the art of negotiation tells of an old oriental carpet dealer whose young son asks "How much is one and one?"

"It all depends," the father responds. "Are you buying or selling?"

The more you think about prices the more you will realize that every price is negotiable. The price of anything depends upon your relative need to have something balanced against the seller's need to dispose of that same item.

Price also depends upon the relative knowledge of the parties. **Lease On Your Terms** will give you much of the knowledge you need in order to negotiate on equal terms with your landlord.

NEGOTIATING AND MOVING ARE STRESSFUL

All things change. We live in a world of rapid change and relate to change admirably. During our lifetimes we have seen all kinds of changes from horse drawn vehicles to space travel. we easily accept all kinds of changes except where the change affects our income or living conditions. Changes on the job and changes of residence account for two of the most stressful of life's stressful passages. Psychologists say the death of a loved one, discovering terminal illness and conviction of a crime are probably the only things more stressful than your landlord changing his lease (because it affects his income) and you changing your residence (because it involves a change of life style).

Talk to your landlord about the mutual stresses you are experiencing and try to accommodate your mutual needs and desires by meaningful trade offs in the lease negotiation process.

WE ARE NOT A FIXED PRICE ECONOMY

Sellers like to perpetuate a myth that we are a fixed price economy.

To some degree fixed prices are a necessity. They speed up most commercial transactions. Who wants to wait on a long line at the A&P, while every person ahead of you attempts to negotiate the purchase of each item? But even the A&P marks down items that are perishable for same day sale. Moreover, you can stock up when the A&P offers sale items at loss leader prices as an inducement for you to shop there.

Many prices for many items such as train tickets, telephone calls and utility bills are set by tariff and regulated by governmental bodies such as the Metropolitan Transit Authority, the Public Service Commission and the like.

The prices of most items, however, such as the prices charged by Sears and the A&P are regulated by competition. People tend to shop where the prices and quality are best.

THE LAW OF SUPPLY AND DEMAND

On a broader level there are economic laws of supply and demand which govern general prices on a market level. After a lifetime of buying, selling and negotiating, **Lease On Your Terms** has concluded that you, as one consumer, almost never have to worry about those iron laws of supply and demand for several reasons:

1. There is a vast market of producers who respond to demand by over-producing until the supply exceeds the demand and the price drops to a point where production is no longer profitable.

2. You are always involved in a local market where the buyers and sellers are usually evenly matched.

3. Even in a total sellers market like the New York City apartment rental market in the era of the 1980s, yuppies and renters had options like taking in roommates or moving to the less crowded suburbs.

4. There is always someone under greater compulsion to sell then you are to buy. After all, people are continually dying, divorcing, moving, retiring, getting fired, suffering adversity, upgrading and the like. You just have to be creative and find your most desperate seller.

5. Remember that there are always options.

6. Always look for bargains.

UNDERSTANDING YOUR LANDLORD'S NEEDS

In order to negotiate with your landlord you have to understand your landlord's needs, priorities and desires. Once you satisfy your landlord's basic needs and expectations, it is easier to negotiate a more evenly balanced lease. **Many landlord oriented clauses in the lease are unnecessary for the landlord's basic needs. A reasonable landlord should be willing to trade off those unnecessary clauses for more reasonable terms. After all, your landlord is competing for good tenants and should be willing to accommodate your reasonable needs.**

NEED FOR PROMPT PAYMENT OF RENT

The very first need of the landlord is the prompt payment of rent on the due date. Your landlord has his own expenses to meet including a mortgage owed to the bank. The bank has the same late charges and penalties built into its mortgage that the landlord has built into the lease.

LANDLORD'S NEED TO PRESERVE AND PROTECT THE PREMISES

The second need of the landlord is the return of the rented premises in the same condition as originally rented to you, except for reasonable wear and tear. Your landlord has substantial capital investment in the rented premises. Capital is an economic term for that which you have not consumed and have saved for the future. Savings and investments are the normal form in which capital is held today.

Capital is the world's greatest coward. Consider the manner in which you cherish and treat your own savings. You want to protect and preserve your capital for you future needs. The rented premises represent the landlord's savings and investment. He wants this investment protected by you: your obligation under the lease is to take generally good care of the rented premises.

LANDLORD'S NEED TO UNDERTAKE NO FURTHER LIABILITY

The third need of the landlord is not to undertake any additional responsibility or liability to third persons by your actions. For example, if you tell the landlord that your hobby is making fireworks, you will never get a lease. The landlord may require you to obtain your own casualty, theft and fire insurance on the residence for his protection as well as yours.

LANDLORD'S NEED TO RUN A QUIET HOUSE

The fourth need of the landlord is to run a quiet house in which all of the tenants live in relative harmony.

Most leases will have ground rules known as "landlord's rules". The landlord's rules become part of the lease. They deal with items such as pets, noise, playing loud music, water beds and the like. Always read the house rules.

Remember that different types of landlord's will have different priorities of needs. A small landlord renting an apartment in the house in which he lives will have a different outlook from a large mobile home park landlord. Try to anticipate and respond to your landlord's visible and apparent needs.

Landlord's rules may be legal so long as they are reasonable. For example, a rule stating that you could not enter your residence after midnight would probably keep the noise level down but would be unreasonable.

Your lease will look like the Ten Commandments. It will be filled with "Thou shall nots". The lease will say "Don't make alterations to the premises. Don't make noise. Don't keep a pet. Don't install an air conditioner or dishwasher or washing machine /dryer. Don't do anything objectionable". After a literal reading of your lease you will feel that all you can do is make your monthly rent payment on time.

Also remember that you can be evicted if you are an objectional tenant, or more to the point, engage in objectional conduct. The landlord will try to show that your conduct constitutes a substantial violation of the lease or house rules. Objectional conduct to the landlord and under your lease will be defined in words indicating behavior which makes or will make the dwelling or the building less fit to live in for you or other occupants. It will also mean anything which interferes with the right of others to properly and peacefully enjoy their units, or causes conditions that are dangerous, hazardous, unsanitary and detrimental to other tenants.

Objectional conduct will be measured by a judge in the light of reasonableness. Your right to enjoy your dwelling will be balanced against the interference to other tenant's rights to enjoy their dwellings and the damages, if any, to the landlord's property.

There is a body of case law in New York that holds that you do have a right to enjoy the use of the premises you have rented. Judges in New York simply do not enforce lease clauses or house rules that require the tenant to live in the 18th century. Judges in New York allow reasonable tenants under reasonable circumstances to keep pets, play music, make alterations, remodel their apartments, and install air conditioning and washer/dryers in spite of lease or house rules to the contrary.

Judges in New York balance the tenants right to live with the harm, if any, to other tenants and to the property of the landlord. In theory, judges will allow you to build bookshelves so long as you remove them when you leave and patch up the walls, if the landlord so requests.

This does not mean that the law of your city or state agree with New York law or that your local judges will also look the other way to minor and literal transgressions under your lease. In theory, a man's home is his castle and you should have the right to use and enjoy your dwelling so long as no one else is harmed or complains. You should be allowed to use your rented premises to enjoy life in all of its rich diversity.

WHAT THE LANDLORD WANTS

Your landlord's bargaining position is quite easy to assess. YOUR LANDLORD WANTS AS MUCH MONEY AS THE MARKET WILL BEAR AND THE LAW WILL ALLOW. AND HE WANTS AS MUCH MONEY PRE-PAID AS THE MARKET WILL BEAR AND THE LAW WILL ALLOW.

BALANCING PRICE, TIME AND LIMITS OF LIABILITY

Once you realize that the United States is not a fixed price economy, it is easy to understand that everything is negotiable. It is usually only a matter of price. Fundamental negotiating techniques are a balancing act in which price, time and dollar limits on liability are balanced against each other.

You may be willing to enter into a longer lease in exchange for a rent reduction. You may be willing to agree to an onerous landlord's clause, provided that the damages under it are limited to a certain dollar limit or time period. For example, you may be willing to be liable for liquidated damages if you move out, provided that the damages do not exceed either $1,000 or two months rent, whichever you feel is better for you or achievable in negotiation.

In the negotiation zone you are always trading off between price, limits upon liability and time.

THE NEGOTIATION ZONE

You have entered the NEGOTIATION ZONE. A dimension not only of time and space, but also of mind, not to mention dollars, cents and common sense. In the NEGOTIATION ZONE you will come face to face with people of incredible greed and will have a chance to realize all of your most secret fears.

But you will also encounter your own secret reserves of inner strength and mental acuity. It is your unknown inner reserves that will enable you to understand your landlord and to satisfy many of your basic needs in your lease.

UNDERSTANDING YOUR OWN NEEDS

According to an old proverb, it is a wise man who knows himself. It is also wise to know and distinguish what you really need from what you want. Most people want everything. The science of economics is concerned with balancing the wants of society as a whole (and individuals in microcosm) with the world's ability to satisfy those wants. As you would expect, wants always exceed needs.

You must examine your real and urgent needs and the resources at your disposal to satisfy those needs. In negotiations with your landlord you can not reasonably expect to achieve all of your goals because some of them conflict with the landlord's goals and with the general market conditions. For example, you may want the lowest possible rent, while the landlord wants the highest possible rent. Fortunately, the prevailing market conditions for rents of comparable dwellings will set reasonable boundaries for each of you. You can start negotiations at the low end of the spectrum while the landlord starts at the upper end. Hopefully, you will meet somewhere after trading off for other items each of you need.

Lease On Your Terms gives you much more ammunition than you will need. Be judicious in your selection of those riders you really need and hold out for them. You can always change your mind later. ALWAYS KEEP YOUR RELATIVE BARGAINING POSITION IN MIND.

THE CALCULUS OF PROBABILITIES

How do you decide which of the Tenant's clauses you wish to add as riders to the landlord's proffered standard form of lease? It is an axiom that all clauses are not created equal. Some clauses are more important than others. Which clauses are the most important will depend upon your individual circumstances. Only you can decide what is most likely to happen in your life during the term of your lease.

Lawyers evaluate the important clauses from the unimportant clauses based upon what they call "the calculus of probabilities". Calculus was a form of mathematics developed independently by Sir Isaac Newton in England and Gottfried Liebniz in Europe at the same time in 1687. Calculus is the mathematics of objects moving at different rates of speeds, such as the elliptical orbits of planets when confronted by gravity, or the average speed your car will travel when you proceed from a dead stop and shift through all the gears up to a measured quarter mile.

Probabilities refers to the odds that any given event will occur during the term of the lease. You could die at any time. You have an anticipated life span of 75 years, however, and the probability of your death during the term of the lease may be minimal. Only you know your age, health and habits and are in a position to assess the calculus of probabilities of your dying within the term of the lease.

You must assess the probabilities of any particular event occurring and protect yourself against the most likely possibilities. You can place unlikely contingencies on the bottom of the list. The higher the probability the more you will want to negotiate for the tenant's rider that protects you against that eventuality.

YOUR GOALS IN NEGOTIATION

Several matters are being discussed between you and you landlord. The landlord is sizing you up as a potential tenant and you are wondering if this is the kind of place you want to live in for the foreseeable future. You will be negotiating at least a security deposit of up to two months rent, another months's rent payable in advance, and whether or not to sign a lease and if so, of what duration and containing what terms.

It is important to set realistic goals prior to beginning the negotiation process. If you don't know what you want, how will you know when you've gotten it? Or conversely as Dorothy muses in the land of Oz, if you don't know where you are going, any road can get you there.

You must also set priorities so that you know what is important and what is even more important. Anything less important can be traded off for what you really need.

Your goals and priorities are unique to you. No one else can establish your likes and dislikes and your needs and desires. Your goals and priorities are what make you so individually you.

SET A DOLLAR VALUE ON EACH GOAL

You keep score in negotiating in dollars and cents. You must give each item in the negotiation process and decision process a dollar value. For example, how valuable is a dwelling within walking distance to work when compared to another residence 40 miles distant in the suburbs? How could anyone else make that decision for you and how do you evaluate that decision yourself?

Dollars are the universal solvent and the only constant standard of measure. How much each month is bus and train fare? What will a car cost each month for the commute? How much time will the commute take and what is the value of your time? If you are a lawyer or plumber who bills his time at $250 per hour you will have no problem computing the value of your time.

The **Lease On Your Terms** list of Goals and Priorities Form is set forth below and in the FORMS section of this book.

LIST OF GOALS AND PRIORITIES FORM

LIST OF GOALS	PRIORITY OF EACH GOAL	DOLLAR VALUE OF EACH GOAL
1.		
2.		
3.		
4.		
5.		
6.		

THE ART OF MAKING TRADE OFFS

Just as the landlord does not need all of the landlord's clauses and protection under the lease, you do not need all of the clauses and protection contained in Lease On Your Terms. You and your landlord will each negotiate for those clauses you most need. For example, if you are thinking of changing jobs and may have to relocate, you need a strong assignment or sublet clause and the right to be left off the hook for further damages. Negotiate to limit your damages to a small number of month's rent as liquidated damages should you move. In this manner the landlord takes a crap shoot that it will take him less than that number of months to find a replacement tenant and the landlord gets to keep the profit. You are happy because you have limited your liability to a manageable amount (which may equal your employer's moving allowance) and the landlord is happy because he may turn a profit in a low vacancy market.

Once you have compiled your list of goals and the prioritized value of each goal to you, you are in a position to trade off what you don't really need in exchange for what you actually must have.

DON'T NEGOTIATE AGAINST YOURSELF

Negotiating against yourself means that you change your offer before the landlord changes his position. For example, suppose the landlord is asking $1000 a month in rent. You have counter-offered with $800 based upon your consideration of other equally attractive available residences. Don't increase your offer from $800 until the landlord drops his offer from $1000. Otherwise you are negotiating against yourself in that you are offering more money without getting anything in return.

When you are in a negotiation zone, you should negotiate, negotiate and negotiate. Always write down and review each offer on each open issue made by you and each response or counter offer made by the landlord. By recording each offer and counter offer you insure that you aren't negotiating against yourself.

Lease On Your Terms has developed a Tenant's Offer Sheet which is set forth below and in the FORMS section of this book. The purpose of the Tenant's Offer Sheet is to record each offer and counter-offer. You can start out with the landlord's asking price for rent and then record each new and improved offer.

Then ask about concessions in rent and record them. If the landlord offers one month, you can ask for one month and a paint job and an air conditioner. Once again record each offer of a concession and each counter-offer.

Record your offers and counter-offers loudly and clearly so that you and the landlord are certain as to exactly what shifts in bargaining position have occurred. Nothing is more embarrassing that to think you have a deal and to discover that the other side "never said that".

When you are finished with the bargaining, each of you and the landlord or his agent should sign the Tenant's Offer Sheet so that both of you confirm the present status of the deal.

TENANT'S OFFER SHEET

PREMISES LOCATED AT_____

_____

_____

DATE: _____

NAME OF LANDLORD OR AGENT_____

RENT

FIRST
 OFFER   COUNTER-OFFER

SECOND
 OFFER   COUNTER-OFFER

THIRD
 OFFER   COUNTER-OFFER

CONCESSIONS

FIRST
 OFFER   COUNTER-OFFER

SECOND
 OFFER   COUNTER-OFFER

THIRD
 OFFER   COUNTER-OFFER

_____
Landlord

_____
Tenant

YOU CAN ALWAYS THINK ABOUT THE DEAL OVERNIGHT

Rome wasn't build or destroyed in one day. There is no reason (other than your own desire) to complete a negotiation in one day. You can always sleep on it. Sometimes a deal that looked great the day before can look terrible in the cold, gray light of morning.

One client of the author of **Lease On Your Terms** would never enter into a business deal until he talked the matter over with his father. His father had been dead for over ten years. His aim was to buy time to think and mull and ruminate.

The more you think about anything, the smarter you get. You begin to think about curves and wrinkles, nooks and crannies, and "what ifs" that never occurred to you before. You can begin the next day of negotiations with your new ideas.

OVERCOMING LANDLORD'S OBJECTIONS TO LEASE CHANGES

Landlords don't like tenants' changes to their standard lease for many reasons. They know and understand their standard lease and don't want to learn new experiences. They also prefer standardization in which they can act mechanically with respect to all tenants. Landlords discourage negotiating lease changes with tenants.

Landlords are conservative in both financial and political outlook. Your landlord thinks and acts just like former President Ronald Reagan. Both believe in protecting property rights over people rights. Your landlord has been owning property and risking his assets by allowing strangers use of his property for so long that he knows things never change for the better. Rust never sleeps. Buildings age and decay. All change is for the worst.

Above all he hates lawyers. He knows that lawyers cost money. The secret of happiness to any landlord is a full rent role on the asset side of the balance sheet and not having to make repairs, pay lawyers, doctors or psychiatrists on the liabilities side.

YOU MUST ORIENT YOUR LANDLORD TO CHANGE

In many respects landlords are like a the Chairman of the Board of a bank your author represented who discouraged bank counsel from negotiating changes to the bank's standard lending documents. "If they want my money, they sign my documents," the Chairman used to say in a harsh whisper reminiscent of Marlon Brando in the **Godfather**.

Many landlords will use the same intimidating tactic. "If you want to rent my dwelling, then you sign my lease." Most things in life are subject to the give and take of negotiation. Most deals are not take it or leave it deals. In order to make a deal the financial, emotional and physical needs of each party must be satisfied. Explain this to the "take it or leave it" landlord. Your landlord is competing with all other landlords in the market place. He has to make a deal as much as you do.

The end result of your negotiating strategy will depend upon your relative bargaining strength and position.

DISARMING LANDLORD'S PLOYS

Listed below are several ploys used by landlords to thwart negotiations or changes to their leases and your response (unless of course you have a better answer).

LANDLORD: We never make changes to our lease.

TENANT: The clause I want to change is unreasonable. My proposed change is reasonable. Please tell me right now whether I am dealing with a reasonable person. If you are totally unreasonable, it may affect my desire to have you as a landlord.

LANDLORD: I would never agree to that change.

TENANT: Suppose I offered you $1,000 as an absurd amount of additional rent in exchange for that clause? (Once you have reduced an idea to concrete dollars it becomes easier to agree to the concept of trading one clause for another).

LANDLORD: Why do you need that?

TENANT: Explain why the clause is necessary and why the landlord should be willing to give in on this issue. A more wiseguy approach is to say "I need it for the same reason you don't want to give it to me."

LANDLORD: I will never agree to that. Take it or leave it.

TENANT: Most business deals are not take it or leave it deals. Most commercial transactions are the result of give and take bargaining between the parties. I have reasonable needs that must be satisfied and I am prepared to pay for those needs.

My needs are not handled in your form of lease.

Let's discuss this in a reasonable manner. If you are going to be totally unreasonably now before my money and life style are committed to living with you, what are you going to be and how are you going to act later?

PART 4

MOVING IN PROBLEMS

SECURITY DEPOSIT

In most apartment complexes, the prospective tenant will be asked to pay a security deposit of up to 2 months rent, to pay one month's rent in advance, and to sign a lease. A security deposit is the lump sum that you pay a landlord when you sign a lease. The deposit is like the five cent deposit you pay on a soft drink bottle in certain states. It secures the landlord against any loss of rent caused by your vacating the premises prior to the end of the lease or physical damage you inflict on the premises.

You are supposed to get the security deposit back when you leave provided that you adhere to the lease and cause no damage to the dwelling. At the end of the lease you want your landlord to furnish an itemized list of damages, if any, he claims you have caused to the premises.

Your landlord should not commingle your security deposit with his own funds. In addition, you want your landlord to place your security deposit into a segregated interest bearing bank account.

Under New York State law the landlord must place the security deposit into a segregated account separate from the landlord's own money and inform you of the name of the bank. Your security deposit is treated as a trust fund. It does not belong to the landlord.

Furthermore, under New York law, if your building has six or more apartments, the landlord must place your segregated security deposit into an interest bearing bank account and tell you the name of the bank. Your landlord must also pay the accrued interest to you when he returns the security deposit. The landlord is allowed to keep one percent of the interest as an administrative fee.

Generally, the amount of the security deposit is negotiable. State and local law where you live may limit the amount of the security deposit. Under New York City law, for example, a rent controlled tenant need only post one month's security.

TENANT'S SECURITY DEPOSIT CLAUSE

Landlord agrees to hold tenant's security deposit as trust funds in a segregated interest bearing bank account and to inform tenant of the name and address of the bank where the account is maintained within the next thirty days.

Landlord shall return the security deposit to tenant with all accrued interest when the lease shall have terminated, provided that Tenant has substantially complied with the lease. Landlord may keep one percent of the accrued interest as an administrative fee.

At the end of this lease landlord agrees to render an itemized list of deductions, if any, for damage landlord claims tenant has caused to the premises.

Landlord recognizes that tenant needs the prompt return of the security deposit to use as rent for tenant's next dwelling. Accordingly landlord agrees to return the security deposit or the unused portion thereof to the tenant at the same time that the tenant surrenders the keys to the dwelling to the landlord.

THE BATTLE OF THE FORMS

The next two FORMS should already be in your landlord's vocabulary of standard forms. You want the landlord to receipt and account for all the money you are paying as a security deposit, rent and advance rent under the lease. You should compare the following tenant oriented forms with the landlord's forms in order to protect all of your rights.

IF CERTAIN PROVISIONS OF THE TENANT'S FORMS ARE MORE TO YOUR LIKING, NEGOTIATE, NEGOTIATE AND NEGOTIATE.

GET A RECEIPT FOR YOUR SECURITY DEPOSIT

Don't forget to get a receipt signed by the landlord or his agent for your security deposit. Use the form of Receipt For Security Deposit set forth below and reprinted in the FORMS section at the end of this book.

RECEIPT FOR SECURITY DEPOSIT

RECEIVED from_____

Insert name of Tenant(s) as in the lease

the Sum of $_____

Insert amount of security deposit

as a security deposit in connection with the lease of premises known as

_____

Insert street address of the dwelling

_____.

Insert city, state and zip code of the dwelling

The security deposit shall be returned with all accrued interest when the lease shall terminate, provided that Tenant(s) have substantially complied with the lease. Landlord may keep one percent of the accrued rent as an administrative fee.

Signed _____

Insert name of landlord or agent

ADVANCE RENT

Advance rent is rent that is prepaid by you. The question is whether the advance rent is for the first month or the last month of the lease. You would prefer the first month for cash flow purposes.

The **Tenant's Guide** has included a form of Receipt for Advance Rent set forth below and in the FORMS section of this book.

RECEIPT FOR ADVANCE RENT

RECEIVED From_____
Insert your name

The Sum of $_____
Insert amount of advance rent

as _____ month's (weeks) of advance
Insert number of month's/weeks advance rent

rent in connection with premises known as_____ _

_____.

Insert street, city and zip code address of the dwelling

The advance rent shall be applied to the initial month(s) of the lease.

Signed_____
Insert name of landlord or agent

CONCESSIONS
IN FAVOR OF THE TENANT

It is not unusual for landlords to make concessions to tenants in order to induce tenants to sign a lease. Concessions are any of a number of possible bonuses granted by landlords at their own expense to tenants. For example, ideal concessions include an air conditioner to make an apartment more livable and a fresh paint job.

Other concessions can include free rent, installation of carpeting, new appliances, dish washing machines and just about anything that you can negotiate. Concessions will also depend upon your needs and upon the condition of the premises.

Landlords can be more generous in concessions like appliances, carpeting, bookshelves, wall units and the like which constitute improvements to the residence, because these items belong to the landlord at the end of the lease and can be attractive to the next tenant. On the other hand a rent abatement or forgiveness is a one time item lost to the landlord forever.

The concessions, if any, your landlord is willing to make will depend upon general market conditions and your attractiveness as a tenant. In New York City it was impossible to find an apartment in the go-go days of the 1980s. Today, New York City landlords in many buildings are willing to make substantial concessions. **Lease On Your Terms** has included a Tenant's Concessions Clause set forth below and included in the FORMS section of this book.

TENANT'S CONCESSIONS CLAUSE

Landlord hereby agrees to grant the following concessions to Tenant at landlord's expense:

1. _____

   Insert concessions, i.e., number of month's free rent, air conditioning unit, new paint job, quality of materials, etc.

2. _____

3. _____

4. _____

WORK ORDERS
AT LANDLORD'S EXPENSE

It is not uncommon for the tenant to require certain changes or alterations be made to the premises either before or after the tenant moves in. Alterations could include such items as installation of a window air conditioner or repainting the premises.

Work to be performed by the landlord under the lease should be set forth in a work order appended to the lease. The work order should also state

1. whether the landlord or tenant is to pay for the work

2. the completion date for the work

3. the quality of the materials to be used and

4. what happens if the work is not completed on time.

Furthermore, if a particular standard other than builder's standard is to be used, the work order should so specify. Builder's standard is the cheapest acceptable product available. Accordingly, if you expect a better grade of product, you should specify the brand name and quality you have bargained for.

For example, it the landlord has agreed to paint the outside of a house you have rented, he will use the cheapest paint he can buy wholesale. If you want Sears Weatherbeater or another type of long lasting five year warranted paint, you should identify that paint in the work order.

AT TENANT'S EXPENSE

It is also possible that the landlord will perform work at your expense which you request or desire in order to make the residence more suitable to your needs. Many times when you move into a new town or neighborhood, you are not as familiar with the tradesman and craftsman and the going prices for services as the landlord. Accordingly, it may be beneficial for you to hire the landlord to perform alterations which you desire at your expense.

Lease On Your Terms has inserted the Tenant's Work Order Clause set forth below and in the FORMS section of this book to handle the matter of work orders. NOTE THAT THE TENANT'S WORK ORDER CLAUSE IS DIVIDED INTO TWO PARTS DEPENDING UPON WHETHER THE WORK IS TO BE PERFORMED AT THE LANDLORD'S EXPENSE OR AT YOUR EXPENSE.

TENANT'S WORK ORDER CLAUSE

Landlord agrees to complete for the tenant the work set forth below. Landlord shall use all best efforts to complete the work prior to tenant's move -in date. Landlord agrees that all work on the premises will be completed not later that 30 days after tenant's move-in date.

Landlord agrees to use materials equal to builders' standard unless a higher quality or brand name is set forth below.

Landlord agrees to perform <u>at landlord's expense</u> the work set forth below:

1. Insert itemized list of work to be performed and the quality of materials to be used.

2.

3.

4.

Landlord agrees to perform <u>at tenant's expense</u> the work set forth below:

Insert itemized list of work to be performed and the quality of materials to be used.
1

2.

3.

4.

PAINTING

Will the landlord give you a new paint job in colors suited to your fancy? The answer will be subject to negotiation and/or your local housing maintenance code. YOU MUST CHECK YOUR LOCAL HOUSING MAINTENANCE CODE TO DETERMINE HOW OFTEN YOUR LANDLORD MUST PAINT YOUR DWELLING. THE DISCUSSION THAT FOLLOWS IS MAINLY THE RULE IN NEW YORK CITY.

Under New York City's Housing Maintenance Code the landlord must paint an apartment at least once every three years. However, the landlord and tenant may agree that an additional painting is not required for an additional two years after that.

If your landlord has previously painted the dwelling in one color, that remains his current obligation. The landlord must repaint the entire dwelling in a neutral shade and in a workmanlike manner.

If you painted in your own colors, your landlord has no obligation to follow your color scheme and may use one neutral shade. Also, if you should paint your apartment before the landlord is required to paint, your landlord need not reimburse you.

The landlord is liable for any damage his painters cause to your property. Don't sign any waiver releasing the landlord from such liability. You are under no legal compulsion to sign any waiver of the landlord's liability.

Your landlord's painters have the obligation to move furniture into the middle of the room and cover and protect your personal belongings. It is a good idea for you to move your easy to carry family pictures and valuables yourself into the middle of the room in order to protect them from annoying chips and scrapes.

WALLPAPER

Lease On Your Terms does not want to make a proctologist out of you but wallpaper is a pain in the ass to landlords.

Wallpaper is difficult to put up. It is much more labor intensive than painting. It takes longer to match the patterns of wallpaper than to throw a fresh coat of builder's standard paint on the walls.

Wallpaper is also difficult and time consuming to remove. Often wallpaper rips gouges and holes in plasterboard walls necessitating expensive and time consuming repatching and sizing when you leave.

Furthermore, wallpaper designs are more individualized than paint colors. It is hard to find a neutral shade wallpaper and if you found it, you would find it too boring. Wallpaper tends to be loud and outlandish and too unique to your individual tastes for the next tenant to accept.

Don't affix wallpaper without the landlord's written consent. Under New York law, for example, there is no requirement that the landlord wallpaper the walls or suffer you to paper the walls. If you wallpaper, be prepared to pay for the costs of removing the paper and sizing the wall when you leave. If the landlord consents in writing, then you don't have to remove the paper when you leave.

LANDLORD TO PROVIDE BASIC VITAL INFORMATION

You want the landlord to furnish a list of vital particulars so that you know who to contact in case of emergency.

The less familiar you are with the neighborhood, the more you need to know vital information. After all, the dwelling is in the landlord's turf and he has a reservoir of knowledge from which you can draw.

For example, what is the telephone number of the police and fire departments? The ambulance and paramedic services? The gas, electric, water and cable TV companies.

What is the phone number of the superintendent, janitor, or building manager? How do you call the doorman? How do you call the landlord? Suppose the super is out or on vacation— how do you call an alternate in order to resolve an emergency?

The landlord should share these concerns with you and help you prepare an emergency list for his benefit and for your benefit. For example, where is the fire extinguisher nearest to your dwelling? The main gas shutoff valve? The main or ancillary water shutoff valve?

The Landlord's Vital Information Sheet is set forth below and in the FORMS section of this book.

LANDLORD VITAL INFORMATION SHEET

FOR YOUR INFORMATION:
IMPORTANT TELEPHONE NUMBERS

Landlord's name_____

Landlord's address_____

_____

Landlord's business phone number_____

Landlord's home phone number_____

Police Department_____

Fire Department_____

Ambulance_____

Paramedic Service_____

Doctor_____

Telephone Company_____

Gas Company_____

Electric Company_____

Water Company_____

Cable TV Company_____

Garbage Removal_____

Exterminator_____

Building Manager_____

Landlord_____

Janitor_____

Doorman_____

Plumber_____

Electrician_____

Location of the fire extinguisher nearest your dwelling:

_____

Location of the main electrical shutoff for your dwelling:

_____

Location of the main gas shutoff valve for your dwelling:

_____

Location of the main water shutoff for your dwelling:

_____

Location of garbage and refuse removal cans:

_____

Miscellaneous:

_____

_____

_____

_____

WHEN THE LANDLORD CANNOT DELIVER THE PREMISES

The commencement date of the lease arrives and the landlord tells you that he cannot deliver occupancy of the premises to you. A situation beyond his control might prevent the landlord from letting you move into the premises on the beginning date set in the lease. The old tenant may have refused to move out or has no where to go. Often a game of musical chairs occurs. The prior tenant cannot move as anticipated because of unforeseen circumstances.

This is a particularly vexatious problem. You may have already moved from your old residence in anticipation. Or you must vacate by a date certain or be held for damages. You don't want to be the loser in this game of musical chairs. You are totally innocent and are not the cause of the problem. All you want is the benefit of your bargain under the lease which is the use and occupancy of the rented premises. And you want it NOW.

The standard landlord oriented lease provides that the landlord will not be responsible for your damages or expenses and the lease will remain in effect. Moreover, the landlord can tie you up for a period of time (30 days under the New York Standard Form of Apartment Lease) after which you can then elect to terminate the lease within an additional 15 days

Lease On Your Terms says, "Give me a break." Where are you going to live for 45 days—in your car? In this regard **Lease On Your Terms** has reprinted below excerpts from the National Lampoon article about "The Most Livable Automobiles of 1991".

"Every year a remarkable number of automobiles qualify for the mantle of 'most livable'. And this year is no exception."

"As in years past habitability is still one category where 'Made in U.S.A.' is a credit and not a demerit."

The editors of twenty major car magazines based their voting on a complex set of criteria and, as always, on some personal preferences and prejudices. Points were awarded or subtracted for prestige as well as for comfort.

"This year's results may surprise you.

"Number one was the Ford Aerostar. Arrangible modular seating made this minivan the resounding top choice. Turnable seating in the rear main living area makes it 'perfect' for the 'work-at-home-man.' Points, too, were garnered for the available 'brickface' exterior. The downside? A sloping dashboard makes the Aerostar cabin a poor dining room. Second place Dodge Caravan, with its flat dash and built-in plastic cup holders, was the champion in this category, but lost to Aerostar because it lacked adequate lighting in the master bedroom. Third place Plymouth Satellite station wagon fell from last year's number one spot because, as one editor put it, 'now the basic model is only

available in dark colors. Ever try to sleep in a dark car on a sunny morning? It heats up like...like an oven or something.'

"Rounding out the top four where the Plymouth Sundance coup ('The trunk roof has crossbars perfect for hanging shirts from') and the Infiniti G20 ('Trendy, we know, but that counts for something when you're having the other execs over to work on special projects....Also great air conditioning and tinted windows standard are a plus.')

"The least livable cars? The Celica ST coupe. ('It's not just the nonremovable stick shift in the master bedroom, but the guest bed has a hump down the center, too), the Volvo 940 GLE ('Roll bars aren't that important if you're not driving much'; 'Airbag guest bed hard to refold'), the Cutlass Ciera ('The windows are so high and the doors are so low, there's no privacy'), the Chrysler Fifth Avenue ('You try to make a romantic little fire in the ashtray and the wiring shorts every time'; Unacceptable), and the Suzuki Samurai ('All kidding aside, when you're making a vehicle your primary residence you don't want it flopping over on its side all the time').

"Car's ratings were averaged from the specific ratings in three categories: family, couple and studio/retirement. General hints from the editors of the poll: If you choose an engineless junker, make sure the windows are manual and not power. And when choosing a car as a dwelling, ask yourself: What's it going to look like as an address on an envelope? Can I fulfill my lifestyles goals in this vehicle/domicile? What about romance? What about a family someday? The experts all agree: a less expensive car home may not be a better buy in the long run."

All kidding aside. There is a distinct possibility that the landlord will not be able to deliver the premises to you on the commencement date of the lease. This is particularly disconcerting because the only right you get under the lease is possession of the rented premises. The reasons for non-delivery will allow you to make an informed decision as to waiting for the residence or moving elsewhere. But you want to have the option to decide. You don't want to be bound to the landlord for 45 days or some other insufferably long period if you have nowhere else to live.

You want the ability to do what is best for you. The landlord has already defaulted in his one obligation to you and you must determine what to do. An option is a one way street that goes only in your direction. With an option you can do what is best for you. **Lease On Your Terms** includes a Tenant's Delivery of Premises Clause. This rider compels the landlord immediately to return all of the money you have paid, if the landlord cannot deliver possession of the premises to you on the commencement date or move-in date of the lease. This allows you to find another residence immediately. It also encourages the landlord to expedite his side of the transaction if, for example, the delay is within the landlord's control such as completion of a paint job.

The Tenant's Delivery of the Premises Clause is set forth below and in the FORMS section of this book.

DELIVERY OF THE PREMISES CLAUSE

If the landlord is unable to deliver occupancy of the premises to the tenant on the move-in day or other commencement date of the lease, the landlord shall at tenant's option immediately return to tenant all of the moneys previously paid by tenant hereunder.

It is the express understanding of the landlord and tenant that tenant needs premises in which to live. Accordingly, should landlord for any reason be unable to deliver the premises to tenant, landlord will immediately return all such moneys to tenant so that tenant can find other housing.

Tenant's obligation to pay rent shall begin when tenant actually receives possession of the premises.

TENANT'S MOVE-IN CLAUSE

Once the lease is signed, a binding contract exists. If the tenant backs out at the last moment, he will under most leases forfeit the first month's rent, the security deposit, and may even be liable for monthly rent for the entire term of the lease.

A lot can happen between the time you sign the contract of lease and the time you move in. Your job could be transferred to a different location. You could lose your job or move in with a significant other. You could find a better residence at less cost with better appurtenances and location.

Lease On Your Terms suggests that you negotiate for a clause that limits your damages in the event you chose not to move in after signing the lease. The limitation of damages in this clause gives you great flexibility in your plans at a minimal cost.

Accordingly, your Tenant's Moving In clause limits your damages only to the negotiated number of month's rent and not also the security deposit if you change your mind before you move in.

HOW TO NEGOTIATE THE TENANT'S MOVE-IN CLAUSE

Bear in mind that this is a clause to which you are not entitled unless you have a strong bargaining position. This is not an easy clause for the landlord to live with unless he has a backup tenant.

Your landlord is competing in a world with other landlords in order to attract tenants. The more attractive the lease, the easier to find a tenant.

Your landlord has improved his position by getting a certain number of month's rent for nothing, since you never occupied the residence. Under the law in most states, the landlord has to sue you each month for the defaulted rent. Furthermore, nothing prevents the landlord from finding a back-up tenant in case you decide to walk away.

In any event your landlord will probably find another tenant soon anyway.

The Tenant's Move-In Clause is set forth below and in the FORMS section of this book.

TENANT'S MOVE-IN CLAUSE

If tenant shall notify landlord in writing of tenant's decision not to take possession or move into the rented premises prior to the designated effective date or move-in date, Tenant's liability shall be limited to

_____.

Insert number month's rent

COOLING OFF PERIOD

After signing a contract for any large ticket or stressful item, you sometimes have second thoughts. This is known in the trade as "buyer's remorse". Why did I buy such an expensive car, (coat) (pet) (summer rental house) (vacation trip) _____, _____, (you fill in the blanks).

Another of nature's perversities is that all deals seem to mature at about the same time. You are probably negotiating for several dwellings at the same time. Just as you sign a lease for one, a second even more attractive dwelling becomes available.

You have probably experienced this phenomenon when job hunting. When you seek employment you start out with no job. After several interviews, you still have no job. Then you receive a job offer. It is usually not exactly the job you want, but you rationalize that having a job you don't exactly love is still better than having no job at all. Of course, as soon as you accept the first job offer, the attractive job(s) you really wanted make you offers of employment.

The purpose of the tenant's cooling off period clause is to allow you to sign the first lease that satisfies your minimal needs and still gives you a reasonable time to hear from other prospective landlords who may still be deciding which tenant to accept. For purposes of fairness and reasonableness **Lease On Your Terms** suggests a three business day cooling off period. You may, of course, insert whatever period you require and is reasonable and acceptable to the landlord in the circumstances.

The Tenant's Cooling Off Period Clause is set forth below and in the FORMS section of this book.

TENANT'S COOLING OFF PERIOD CLAUSE

It is expressly agreed between landlord and tenant that notwithstanding any provision in this lease to the contrary, tenant shall have the right to reject this lease for _____ business days after the

Insert number of days

execution and delivery of this lease by tenant. Should tenant exercise this right of rejection, this lease shall be null and void and of no legal significance with the same force and effect as if never signed by the tenant.

All moneys paid by the tenant hereunder shall immediately be returned by landlord to tenant.

PART 5

LIVING UNDER THE LEASE

YOUR RIGHT TO LIVE AS YOU PLEASE

In New Jersey, for example, if the lease has clauses which do not violate any statutory provision but which are unreasonable, the tenant still has recourse. The New Jersey law permits an eviction for breach of a covenant only if the covenant is reasonable. A covenant is another way of saying a promise. Each of the clauses in your lease is a promise. Accordingly, the tenant in New Jersey, is protected from both illegal and unreasonable lease provisions.

In New York City judges recognize that tenants have little bargaining position when signing apartment leases. Accordingly, the judges refuse to uphold the strict tenor of the lease in spite of what the lease says.

Judges in New York City refuse to uphold lease clauses and landlord's rules that provide NO Pets, NO air conditioning, NO washing machines, NO music playing, NO alterations or remodeling to the premises, NO noise, NO sex, and the like. New York judges refuse to evict tenants for mere technical violations of the lease. Judges look for substantial violations.

New York City judges appear to read a rule of reason into every lease. Judges will allow tenants to pursue reasonable activities at reasonable times in spite of prohibitions on such activities in the lease. Judges look to see if there are substantial and substantive harmful effects on any of the other tenants or on the landlord's property before evicting a tenant or compelling a tenant to cease and desist from any action the landlord considers objectionable.

THERE IS NO GUARANTEE THAT THE JUDGES IN YOUR CITY, MUNICIPALITY AND STATE WILL BE AS UNDERSTANDING AND SYMPATHETIC AS NEW YORK JUDGES TO TENANT'S RIGHTS. IT WOULD SEEM THAT YOU HAVE A RIGHT TO LIVE A NORMAL LIFE AS A PRIVATE CITIZEN UNDER YOUR LEASE. IT WOULD ALSO SEEM THAT YOU HAVE A RIGHT TO ENJOY YOURSELF AND TO ENJOY YOUR RESIDENCE FOR ALL OF THE PURPOSES FOR WHICH IT WAS INTENDED AND CAN BE USED FOR HUMAN CONSUMPTION PROVIDED THAT NO ONE ELSE IS HURT OR COMPLAINS.

Remember that your actions will be judged by a rule of reason. What is reasonable to reasonable men and not necessarily what is reasonable to you. If you sleep all day and practice playing the drums after midnight, your neighbors, the landlord and the judge may not find your actions to be reasonable.

The basic rule of thumb is that you are not renting a prison cell or living in a maximum security prison. You have a right to live and enjoy your residence to the fullest of human expectations consistent with the moral and ethical norms of conduct in the 20th and soon to be 21st century.

YOUR RIGHT TO ENJOY YOUR RESIDENCE

AIR CONDITIONING
PETS
DISHWASHER AND LAUNDRY
MUSIC

The substance and intent of the above sub-part dealing with YOUR RIGHT TO LIVE AS YOU PLEASE also applies to YOUR RIGHT TO ENJOY YOUR RESIDENCE.

In short you should have a right to all of the twentieth century comforts your dwelling can hold provided that the wiring and electrical conduit work are sufficient for the added load. This is certainly the New York State rule. Judges in New York will not allow installation of an air conditioning unit or dishwasher or clothes washer or dryer to be deemed a substantial violation of a lease. YOU SHOULD CHECK THE LAW OF YOUR JURISDICTION IN ORDER TO BE CERTAIN.

The rule of reason will apply in New York State to pets and music. So long as your pet is not bothering other residents or damaging the landlord's property, reasonable pets under reasonable control will be allowed by New York Judges. The same rule of reason applies to the playing or rehearsing of music.

THE RENT RECEIPT

Under New York State law a landlord has a duty to provide a written rent receipt. The rent receipt is proof of payment of the rent and the date of payment.

New York makes a slight distinction between (i) rent paid in cash or by any instrument other than the tenant's personal check and (ii) your personal check. Under New York law the landlord must give you a receipt for cash or any instrument (for example a bank or postal money order) except your personal check.

The landlord must give a rent receipt to a tenant who pays by personal check only if the tenant makes a written request for a rent receipt. The theory behind this distinction is that your canceled check serves a your receipt.

The rent receipt should contain the following:
1. The date
2. The amount received by the landlord
3. The identity of the premises and the period for which paid
4. The signature and title of the person receiving the rent.

A sample Tenant's Rent Receipt Form is set forth below and in the FORMS section of this book.

TENANT'S RENT RECEIPT FORM

Date: _____

RECEIVED This day from_____
Insert Your Name

the sum of $_____ as rent for premises known as
Insert the Amount Paid

_____
Insert the Address and Apartment Number

for the period beginning_____
Insert the First Day for which Rent Was Paid

and ending_____
Insert the Last Day for which Rent Was Paid

or for the month (week) of _____
Insert Month or Week

_____
Signed

_____
Title

TENANT'S RIGHT TO SUBLEASE OR ASSIGN

EXISTING LAW DOESN'T WORK

No part of landlord and tenant law seems to be more fraught with uncertainty than the law of sublease or assignment. The law in this area is so confusing that **Lease On Your Terms** is going to paint big picture broad brush strokes. You must check your local jurisdiction state and municipal law concerning sublease and assignment.

Lease On Your Terms's solutions here are totally consensual. They depend upon you and your landlord consenting to the lease clauses allowing you to sublet. Your landlord may or may not wish to consent in advance to being reasonable about your right to sublet depending upon (i) the strength of the local market, (ii) the landlord's relative bargaining power and (iii) the provisions of the local law relating to subleasing.

First a brief word on the economics of subletting and assignment relating to landlord thinking. In a tight rental market with escalating and increasing rents, your landlord doesn't want you competing with him and sub-renting his premises at a profit. He wants his unit back to rent again at a higher rent. In a declining rental market your landlord doesn't want to release your liability for the rent in case your replacement subtenant doesn't pay.

Let's look at the same problem from the tenant's point of view. Two possible scenarios exist. There is the returning tenant and the fleeing tenant. The returning tenant really wants to return to the premises after a sabbatical elsewhere. Suppose you want to spend one year living in Europe and then return to your old residence. The fleeing tenant has no desire to return but wants to reduce his liability for rent for the duration of the lease.

Existing landlord-tenant law relating to assignment and subleasing does not seem to marry the desires and needs of the landlords and tenant very well. Under New York law, for example, in most cases involving assignment and sublease the landlord is obliged to act reasonably. If the landlord doesn't act reasonably, the tenant wins in either assigning or subleasing.

THE PROBLEM IS TIMING; NO ONE WANTS TO WAIT UNTIL AFTER A LONG LAWSUIT TO KNOW IF HE IS CAN ASSIGN OR SUBLEASE A DWELLING — CERTAINLY NOT THE REPLACEMENT TENANT.

Accordingly, the tenant usually fares poorly under either a purported assignment or sublease to a third party. The third party wants certainty. If you are standing in quicksand, no third party wants to stand on your shoulders or hang around and see if you go under. The proposed subtenant or assignee will make other more concrete plans rather quickly. No one will hang around until you and your landlord get done slugging out in the courts whether the landlord was acting reasonably or not.

For this reason **Lease On Your Terms** has addressed this issue on a consensual basis so that you and your landlord can negotiate for your respective rights in advance. When you sign the lease, you may have no idea as to whether you better fit the returning tenant scenario or the fleeing tenant scenario. If you are unsure, you will want to negotiate for the right to do both return and flee.

The Tenant's Assignment Clause is set forth below and in the FORMS section of this book.

DIFFERENCES BETWEEN SUBLEASING AND ASSIGNING

When you sublease you become a landlord. You are now leasing your residence to a new subtenant. You are still liable for all payments under your lease to your landlord whether or not your subtenant pays you. In effect, you are in the returning tenant scenario.

When you assign your lease you are discharged and released from the payment of rent (as envisioned by **Lease On Your Terms**). In effect you are the fleeing tenant in the above scenario.

TENANT'S ASSIGNMENT CLAUSE

Tenant shall have the right to assign this lease subject to the written consent of the landlord. Landlord agrees not to unreasonably withhold consent to such assignment. Any assignee with a net worth and credit standing equal to or in excess of the tenant's shall presumptively be deemed to be an acceptable assignee.

Any assignment hereunder shall be effective _____ days after the tenant shall have notified
Insert number
landlord of the proposed assignment along with a copy of the proposed assignee's net worth statement and Consumer Credit Report. In the event of any such assignment, the original tenant shall be released from the lease and a novation shall be deemed to have occurred.

ASSIGNMENT FORM

In order to assign the lease you will need to use a Form of Assignment. Use the Tenant's Form Of Assignment to assign all of your rights and liabilities under the lease to your replacement tenant. **Lease On Your Terms** has prepared a Form of Assignment set forth below and in the FORMS section of this book.

TENANT'S FORM OF ASSIGNMENT

For value received the undersigned, as tenant under a certain lease, between the undersigned and _____

_____
    Insert name and address of landlord

_____,

as landlord, relating to premises situate and known as

_____
    Insert address of premises to be assigned

_____

_____

(the "premises") hereby assigns all of the right, title and interest in and to the lease of the undersigned for the premises to

_____
    Insert name and address of person(s) to whom the lease is to be assigned

_____

_____

A true and correct copy of the lease is attached hereto. This assignment is subject to the consent of the landlord which consent cannot be unreasonably withheld under the terms of the lease. The assignee hereby agrees to accept all liabilities under the lease.

_____
Tenant —Insert your name

_____
Insert your street address

_____
Insert your city, state and zip code

_____
Insert Name and Address of Assignee

_____

_____

TENANT'S RIGHT TO SUBLEASE

In order to have the right to sublease you will need the Tenant's Sublease Clause set forth below and in the FORMS section of this book.

TENANT'S SUBLEASE CLAUSE

Tenant shall have the right to sublease the premises subject to the written consent of the landlord . Landlord agrees not to unreasonably withhold consent to such subleasing. Any subleasee with a net worth and credit standing equal to or in excess of the tenant's shall presumptively be deemed to be an acceptable tenant. Any sublease hereunder shall be effective _____ days after the tenant shall have notified
Insert number
landlord of the proposed sublease along with (i) a copy of the proposed assignee's net worth statement, (ii) a copy of the proposed assignee's Consumer Credit Report, (iii) the written consent of any cotenant or guarantor of the lease and (iv) a copy of the proposed sublease.

NOTE THAT YOU WILL NEED A PROPOSED SUBLEASE. **LEASE ON YOUR TERMS** SUGGESTS THAT YOU START WITH A PHOTOCOPY OF YOUR LEASE. WHITE WASH OUT THE NAMES AND ADDRESSES OF THE LANDLORD AND TENANT. REPLACE THOSE NAMES AND ADDRESSES WITH YOUR NAME AND NEW ADDRESS AS LANDLORD AND THE PROPOSED SUBTENANT'S NAME AS TENANT.

LANDLORD'S ENTRY TO DWELLING

After the lease is signed and you move in, your landlord still has a continuing interest in your dwelling. The landlord may be responsible for repairs to your residence and to the common pipes and conduits in and through the walls and ceilings. Repairs can also be of an emergency nature. Suppose a broken water pipe in your dwelling is cascading water into the unit below.

The landlord also has a continuing financial interest in the dwelling because he may wish to refinance his mortgage, sell the building, or show your dwelling to prospective tenants for your unit or a similar unit in the building.

You want to harmonize your landlord's rights to enter the premises with your quiet enjoyment of the occupancy of the premises. You would like as much advance notice of entry as possible. You don't want the landlord or his agents popping about your home when you are not there or even worse, when you are there.

In those situations where the landlord has made an appointment with a banker, potential purchaser or prospective tenant, it will be possible for the landlord to give you advance notice. In fact, the landlord probably wants to give you as much notice as possible so that the dwelling is spruced up a bit.

In emergencies it will be every man for himself. You can have no reasonable objection to the landlord or his agent, super, or janitor entering your dwelling to make emergency repairs. Ordinary maintenance should not constitute an emergency. Your landlord should be able to give you notice of normal repairs and routine maintenance.

Lease On Your Terms has included a Notice of Entry form set forth below and in the FORMS section of this book.

NOTICE OF ENTRY

Dear Tenant:

RE: ADVANCE NOTICE OF ENTRY

Reference is made to premises situate at

_____

_____

Insert tenant's address

_____.

Please take notice that the landlord or his designee intends to enter your premises on

_____199__

Insert date

at or about_____(AM) (PM)

for the purpose of_____

_____

Insert purpose of entry

_____

It is anticipated that they will stay approximately_____ (Hours : Minutes).

Insert amount of time

Your presence is not necessary unless otherwise stated herein. Should you not be available to open the door, a pass key will be used for entry.

Thank you for your cooperation.

_____
Landlord

SHUT DOWN OF SERVICES

Periodically, it may be necessary for the landlord to stop, reduce or curtail essential services such as hot and cold running water, heat and elevator services. Normal tests and maintenance may require that the boiler or heating plant be shut down.

Assuming that the landlord is not harassing you, these occurrences are beyond the landlord's control and beyond your control. Minimum inconvenience is the price you pay for living in a developed nation. Normally, you are entitled to no reduction in rent and must grin and bear it. There are times, however, that you may want to make alternate plans. If the landlord knows that the water is going to be turnedoff tomorrow morning, you will also want to know it in advance. Advance knowledge will enable you to cool some water in the refrigerator in case you get thirsty. Forewarned is forearmed.

The Tenant's Guide has prepared a Notice of Shut Down of Services form for you to give to your landlord in advance. This way the landlord can notify you in advance of anticipated shut downs. You will not be caught short and can plan ahead. You may want to deliver several copies of this form to your landlord for his use under the lease.

The Tenant's Notice Of Shut Down Of Services Form is set forth below and in the FORMS section.

NOTICE OF SHUT DOWN OF SERVICES

Dear Tenant:

RE: NOTICE OF SHUT DOWN OF SERVICES

DATE:_____

Reference is made to premises situate at _____

_____
Insert address and unit number

_____.

Please take notice that there will be a curtailment of services as set forth below:

DATE AND TIME _____

NATURE OF SERVICE(S)_____

_____

_____

ANTICIPATED DURATION OF OUTAGE_____(DAYS) (HOURS)

_____
Landlord

UNCONSCIONABLE CLAUSES

An "unconscionable clause" is a term or provision in a lease that is so outrageous that it shocks the conscience of the court. Shocks the conscience of the court means that the judge will refuse to allow the landlord to enforce such a brutal clause. Twentieth century judges have recognized that landlords have greater bargaining power than tenants. The landlord's advantage forces tenants to sign leases with clauses that are disturbingly one-sided to the landlord's benefit.

The doctrine of unconscionability is an attempt of the law to place tenants in legal parity with landlords. The concept is that once a landlord-tenant relationship exists, the stronger party (always the landlord) should not take extremely unfair advantage of the weaker tenant. Judges will sparingly apply this doctrine flexibly after reviewing all of the facts and circumstances of the case.

Under New York law if a court finds any lease or clause in a lease unconscionable at the time it was made, the court may refuse to enforce the lease. The court may also enforce the remainder of the lease without the unconscionable clause. Or the court may limit the application of any unconscionable clause so as to avoid any unconscionable result.

Usually a hearing has to be held to afford the parties a reasonable opportunity to present evidence as to the setting, purpose and effect of that portion of the lease the party believes is unconscionable. WHEN YOU ARE AT THE HEARING STAGE, YOU SHOULD HAVE A LAWYER REPRESENTING YOUR INTERESTS.

REPAIRS

Your landlord probably has a duty under the lease and state and local law to make repairs to the premises.

Repairs are the most vexatious problems to live with under a lease. The landlord won't repair anything unless he has an affirmative obligation to do so. This obligation comes either from the lease or from the law.

Rest assured that the landlord will try to subvert his duty to repair by blaming you. The landlord's first line of defense is that the tenant broke it intentionally or by carelessness and negligence.

As usual the **Lease On Your Terms** solution to the repair problem is consensual. This means that you and your landlord each consent in advance as to who is responsible for repairs, the type of repairs and the dollar threshold under which you will make the repairs. Be prepared to negotiate, unless state or local law force the landlord to make all repairs.

A clause compelling the landlord to make repairs is like chicken soup—it couldn't hurt to have it in your lease. **Lease On Your Terms** has included a Tenant's Repairs Clause which is set forth below and in the FORMS section of this book. Under this clause, as presently drafted, the landlord agrees to make all repairs to the dwelling. When you show this clause to the landlord, his response will certainly tell you where you stand. Unless your state and local law are heavily in your favor, be prepared to negotiate.

TENANT'S REPAIRS CLAUSE

Landlord shall be responsible for all repairs to the dwelling.

HOW TO GET THE LANDLORD TO MAKE REPAIRS

The question of necessary repairs ties in with the landlord's warranty of habitability. See the discussion in **Lease On Your Terms** concerning the landlord's warranty of habitability. The end result of the landlord's failure to make repairs may be a rent rebate action or a withholding of the rent.

For the moment, let's assume that the only reason the landlord hasn't made the repairs is that he doesn't know anything is wrong. You must notify the landlord of the defect that needs repair and give him a reasonable amount of time in which to complete the repairs.

Lease On Your Terms has included a Notice of Defect Letter set forth below and in the FORMS section of this book.

TENANT'S NOTICE OF DEFECT LETTER

_____
Insert date

Re: Notice of Defect

_____
Insert name of landlord or agent

_____
Insert street address of landlord

_____
Insert city, state and zip code

Dear Landlord:

This will confirm the conversation we had today concerning defects in and necessary repair(s) to the dwelling of the undersigned. As you were informed, the following work needs to be done:

_____
Itemize repairs that must be made.

_____

_____

_____

I am relying upon you to make the repairs in a reasonable time and before further damage and possible harm can occur.

Very truly yours,

_____
Insert your name

_____
Insert your street address

_____
Insert your city, state, zip code

THE FOLLOW UP LETTER

After you send the first notice of defect letter, chances are nothing happens. The landlord either does nothing or intends to do nothing. If there is no life threatening emergency, there is time to nail down the landlord's position by sending a follow up letter.

The follow up letter is a bit nastier and threatening than the first notice letter. You want to document that the landlord is refusing to honor his obligation to effect repairs.

The Tenant's Follow Up Notice Letter is set forth below and in the FORMS section of this book.

TENANT'S FOLLOW UP NOTICE LETTER

_____

Insert date

Re: Landlord's failure to repair

_____

Insert name of landlord or agent

_____

Insert landlord's street address

_____

Insert landlord's city, state and zip code

Dear Landlord:

Reference is made to my prior communications to you concerning defects in and necessary repairs to my residence. You will recall that the following repairs must be made in order to make my residence habitable (Insert an itemized list of necessary repairs) :

_____

_____

_____

_____

_____

_____

_____

The situation is getting worse by the passage of time and is bound to deteriorate even further. In the meantime, my standard of living is eroding and my physical security is imperiled.
The provisions of my lease with you and applicable state and local law require you to effectuate repairs.
I do not know what to do next. However, I would like to know that my rent payments will be used to keep my residence in good repair and to prevent injury to me, my family and the general public.
If I do not hear from you presently, I shall have to take whatever action is necessary in order to pursue all of my rights.

Very Truly Yours,

_____

Insert your name

_____

Insert your street address

_____

Insert your city, state and zip code

HOW TO COMPEL THE LANDLORD TO MAKE REPAIRS

Let's assume that you have been more than patient and have written the Notice of Defect and the Follow Up Letter set forth above to your landlord. No action has yet been taken by the landlord. What do you do now?

Lease On Your Terms cannot advise you without knowing much more. So much depends upon the emergency nature of the repair and the threat it poses to human life, occupancy and public safety. Many reasonable options are open to you depending upon the specific facts and circumstances.

If this defect affects many tenants in the same premises, such as lack of heat in the winter, you could:

1. band together in a tenant's association (see below),

2. hire one attorney to represent all of you,

3. Pay rent into the registry of the local court until the landlord makes the repairs.

4. Ask the court to authorize you to use the rent payments on deposit in the court to implement the necessary repairs.

5. Ask the court to appoint a receiver to manage the building and make the repairs.

6. Do many other clever things depending on the local law of your jurisdiction.

This looks like a good time to retain local legal advice. Hire a lawyer or talk to the clerk of the court where you reside. Call legal aid, if necessary.

Your rights, conduct and actions will be determined in large part by the procedural and substantive law of the jurisdiction where you live. But don't despair. There are laws and procedures to resolve repair problems quickly and effectively. This is not the first time landlords have failed to repair premises in your jurisdiction and the lawyers, judges and court clerks will know exactly what to do.

INSURANCE

The landlord may require you to maintain your own personal property and casualty insurance and to make the landlord an additional insured under the policies. Remember that landlords don't want to undertake additional risk. If someone slips, falls or gets injured in your residence, the landlord wants your insurance policy to protect the landlord from damages.

Lease On Your Terms can't get too upset by reasonable insurance requirements. They are for your protection as well. When discussing insurance you must consider two interweaving concepts. One concept is the risks, calamities, casualties and catastrophes you are insured against. The second concept is the dollar threshold of insurance coverage you require to cover your needs.

The insurance you need includes personal property and casualty insurance. Each of these will be discussed below. The dollar amount of coverage depends upon your needs and requirements. **Lease On Your Terms** recommends that you consult with your own insurance agent as to the exact risks covered and the dollar amounts.

Personal Property Insurance

Personal property insurance is called a Homeowners-Tenant's Policy. Old timers refer to it as the HO-4 policy.

THE MOST IMPORTANT CONSIDERATION IS TO BE SURE THAT YOUR PERSONAL PROPERTY POLICY COVERS "ALL RISKS" FOR "ALL PERILS" OTHER THAN RISKS SPECIFICALLY EXCLUDED IN THE POLICY. This is the best coverage you can obtain.

Read and consider those risks specifically excluded. It may be possible to purchase additional extensions of insurance to include those risks you want covered. If your dwelling is next to the Atlantic Ocean in hurricane season, you may be advised to get additional insurance coverage.

Types of coverage under this policy will include fire, theft and all other included risks. Your policy should cover your costs of staying in a hotel, if your dwelling burns down.

There are several extensions or additional coverage you may want to think about. If you have a valuable stamp collection, gun collection, silverware, jewelry, engagement rings or the like, you may want to buy a separate endorsement or "floater". The "floater" will specifically cover those items against loss or theft.

Another extension can cover off-premises theft. If you carry sports equipment, your bicycle, camera, camcorder and the like or go on frequent business trips, you may want this coverage.

How Much Personal Property Insurance Do You Need?

YOU NEED A HIGH ENOUGH DOLLAR AMOUNT OF COVERAGE TO REPLACE ALL OF YOUR PROPERTY. MAKE SURE YOUR POLICY IS KEYED TO "REPLACEMENT COST" OF YOUR PROPERTY. This is the best coverage you can buy.

The cheaper alternative that the insurance companies will try to palm off is to pay you the "actual cash value" of your property. The term "actual cash value" has a deceptive, beguiling and compelling ring. Don't be fooled by it and shop around for the "replacement cost" formula.

The difference in dollars and cents operates as follows. That beautiful leather couch you bought several years ago for $2,000 has a replacement cost today of $3,000, but a depreciated "actual cash value" of $150 in the eyes of the insurer's appraiser.

Take pictures of your possessions and personal property. You can use a regular camera or a camcorder. In either case store the photographs and negatives in a safe deposit box or place other than your dwelling. If the dwelling burns down or gets destroyed, so will pictures stored in the dwelling.

Casualty

Casualty insurance protects you if someone slips, falls or is otherwise injured in your dwelling. At least $100,000 "per occurrence" or "each occurrence" is the standard minimum casualty insurance you would want.

If you also own a car, **Lease On Your Terms** recommends that you buy an "umbrella liability policy" which will tie together your home insurance with your auto insurance. Surprisingly enough, excess insurance coverage is relatively inexpensive once you have the basic coverage. The cost of one million dollars of excess umbrella coverage could be well under $200 a year depending upon your history and circumstances.

Miscellaneous

READ THE POLICY BEFORE YOU BUY IT. Most people don't read the policy until they have a claim. If you don't understand the policy, have your insurance agent explain it to you. Many policies are written in plain English today.

CHECK THE DEDUCTIBLES. Insurance companies don't normally pay the first dollar of loss. You have to absorb a certain amount of loss before you have a claim. For example, the deductible on theft loss may be $250. This means that the first $250 of the loss is yours. Also cost out the extra premium expense for lower deductibles. It may well be worth carrying higher deductibles to protect you from catastrophic loss, if you can afford to eat the higher deductible.

ALWAYS ASK ABOUT DISCOUNTS. The insurance company may not tell you. Many companies give discounts for fire alarms, smoke detectors, fire extinguishers and other incidentals. If you don't ask, you won't find out.

ALWAYS ASK ABOUT EXTENSIONS OR ADDITIONAL COVERAGE. They are other insurance clauses for coverage you may find attractive. For example, additional personal property insurance coverage may be offered for college students living away from home. This coverage may be advantageous to you. Once again, if you don't ask, you won't know.

In any event, **Lease On Your Terms** has attempted to draft an insurance clause for the minimum coverage for the average person of modest means. This may not be you, so please don't hesitate to get independent advice from your own insurance agent. Also, note that the Tenant's Insurance Clause set forth below and in the FORMS section of this book does not include personal property insurance coverage. Personal property insurance is for your benefit and not for the landlord's.

It is ok to add the landlord as an additional insured on your casualty insurance, if the landlord so requests.

The Tenant's Insurance Clause is set forth below and in the FORMS section of this book.

TENANT'S INSURANCE CLAUSE

Tenant shall maintain casualty insurance coverage of at least $100,000 per occurrence.

NOTICES

PERSONAL SERVICE OF NOTICE

You want to be sure that official notices under the lease are delivered in a manner calculated to give actual notice.

The best method of insuring actual notice is personal delivery of the writing to the receiving party with a signed receipt by the party served or a suitable agent. In addition the person physically serving the notice should also note the day, time and the person served and a physical description of the person served.

SERVICE BY MAIL

The best and the worst manner in which to give notice is certified mail, return receipt requested. It is the best way, because the return receipt is signed and dated so the party issuing the notice has proof of receipt and the date of actual delivery. It is the worst manner to give notice because you may have to take a day off from work in order to sign for the certified letter at the Post Office.

Your mailperson will not leave a certified letter in your mail box.

Lease On Your Terms has handled this problem by requiring official notices under the lease to be furnished by personal service or dual mailing. The mail service should be certified mail, return receipt requested with a second copy to be mailed by ordinary first class mail. This insures that you will receive actual notice. Normally the act of mailing a notice constitutes delivery of the notice whether or not actually received. Under strict statutory construction if you have ten days to cure a default, technically the ten days begin to run when the letter is mailed and not when you receive the notice which could be three or four days later.

Most states have a presumption that any item mailed is delivered. **Lease On Your Terms** finesses this problem by providing that notices are not effective until actually received.

The Tenant's Notices Clause is set forth below and in the FORMS section of this book.

TENANT'S NOTICES CLAUSE

Notices required to by given under this lease shall be delivered by personal service or sent certified mail, return receipt requested, with a second copy sent by ordinary first class mail in a postage prepaid, properly addressed envelope.

Notices shall be deemed effective when actually received.

NO TIE IN DEALS OR PRIVILEGES

New York has a law going back to the turn of the century prohibiting any landlord from selling exclusive franchises to any seller of fuel, ice or food to sell or deliver fuel, ice or food to the persons occupying any apartment house, tenement, or bungalow colony.

Apparently, in the old days, the ice man would provide the iceboxes free to the landlords for the privilege of having sole access to sell ice to the premises, presumably at outrageous prices.

Lease On Your Terms would look closely at any tie in deal by which the landlord forces you to buy goods or services from any person. Bear in mind that the landlord does have a recognizable and legitimate interest in designating persons authorized to make repairs to and probably paint the rented premises.

One should differentiate between illegal tie in deals and the landlord's legitimate interest in selecting those trades people who will repair and repaint the premises in what the landlord believes is a workmanlike manner.

PART 6

LEASE RENEWAL PROBLEMS

UNCONSCIONABLE RENT INCREASES

New Jersey law allows a tenant to raise the defense that a rent increase is unconscionable. The legislature sought to give tenants in municipalities which had not adopted rent control some protection from exorbitant rent increases. At least one New Jersey court has held that the landlord bears the burden of proving that the rent increase is not unconscionable.

Factors to be considered when unconscionability is in issue include:

When was the last rent increase?

What was the Consumer Price Index differential in percentages of rent since the last rent increase?

What are the comparable housing costs of existing rentals in the area?

TENANT'S ASSOCIATIONS

Under modern thinking your landlord should not be able to evict you or fail to renew your lease based upon participation in a tenants' association. Your landlord should not be able to terminate or refuse to renew your lease based upon your desire to organize the other tenants into united activities, even if those activities are directed against the landlord.

New York, for example, has a law guaranteeing the right of tenants to form, join or participate in tenants' groups. The New York law prohibits landlords from interfering with the lawful activities of any group, committee or other organization formed to protect tenants' rights.

Furthermore, the landlord is prohibited from harassing, punishing, penalizing, diminishing, or withholding any right, benefit or privilege of a tenant for exercising such right.

Tenants' groups, committees or organizations also have the right to meet in any location on the premises devoted to the common use of all tenants so long as they do not obstruct access to the premises. This usually means the lobby or a game room or meeting room, if any.

Lease On Your Terms has not researched whether tenants' groups are legal in your jurisdiction. You must check this out. We would be surprised to find that tenants' groups are illegal anywhere. This kind of stuff went out with the death of Senator Joseph McCarthy and blacklisting. In the final analysis you have a Constitutional right to free speech and free association. These rights are protected by the First Amendment to the United States Constitution. No court and no judge should dare to rule against you.

Under New Jersey law, for example, the tenants' association has standing to sue the landlord, if it has a sufficient stake in the outcome and adverseness and common problems exist. In New Jersey a tenants' association can incorporate as a non-profit corporation or if it has seven or more members sue as an unincorporated association.

NO RETALIATORY EVICTIONS

Retaliatory evictions are on the cutting edge of change. At common law the landlord could dispossess a tenant for any reason or for no reason. Under modern thinking your landlord cannot retaliate for your attempts to have the dwelling repaired by refusing to renew your lease.

Under New York law today retaliatory evictions are unlawful. The old strategy was that the landlord would refuse to renew your lease and then evict you as a holdover tenant. Today, retaliatory eviction is a defense to a holdover proceeding in New York. No judge is going to evict a tenant for attempting to have the premises repaired in accordance with building and housing maintenance code standards.

The overwhelming need for public safety protects tenants from spiteful evictions. The author of **Lease On Your Terms** remembers living as a child in buildings where tenants were afraid to assert their legal rights for fear that the landlord would throw parents and their children into the streets when the lease ended by its terms. The legal theory is that if tenants who file housing code violations can get evicted for reporting the violations, no one would report the violations and the landlords would be able to circumvent the law.

A WORD OF CAUTION. HIRE A LAWYER TO DEFEND YOUR RETALIATORY EVICTION CASE. GO TO LEGAL AID, IF NECESSARY.

PROPERTY TAX INCREASES AND REBATES

Your landlord will want to pass along any real estate tax increases to you under the lease or at lease renewal time. Unless your rent is regulated by state or municipal regulations such as New York City's rent control or rent stabilization, your landlord will want to pass tax escalations through to you.

Tax increases are usually a problem in multi-year leases. Your landlord knows his taxes for the first year of the lease and has fixed the rent with knowledge of his real estate taxes. Accordingly, you want to use year one as the base period and only pay your share of tax increases after the first year. In other words you don't want to know about a real estate increase in year one of your lease.

In years two and three of your lease tax increases can be a problem. Your landlord wants to protect his bottom line income from increased expenses such as taxes and will most assuredly have a mechanism to pass tax increases through to you.

What goes up must come down. Just as the landlord wants to pass tax increases through to you, you want the landlord to pass tax rebates and property tax reductions back to you. IT ALL DEPENDS UPON YOUR NEGOTIATING STRENGTH AND SOMETIMES YOUR LOCAL LAW. Property tax savings result from state wide and municipal wide reevaluations of real estate and from lower school taxes. These rebates are generated by the government itself.

There are instances where the landlord brings his own tax certiorari action against the state or local government to lower the taxes on his property.

Rent rebates for property tax decreases is not so crazy an idea. In New Jersey, for example, there is a Tenant Property Tax Rebate Act which requires the landlord to provide a property tax rebate to the tenants for each year in which the landlord receives a property tax rebate. The property tax reduction may be credited as a rent reduction or paid directly to the tenant.

Your landlord should have no problem in agreeing to pass tax rebates through to you. If he wants the rent increases to cover tax increases, he should be prepared to share the reductions. His only legitimate response is that he should be allowed to recoup any attorneys' fees he has paid in connection with tax certiorari proceedings. In tax cert cases, the landlord has fought to have the taxes lowered for his individual benefit.

Your jurisdiction probably has no law like the New Jersey statute. Accordingly, **Lease On Your Terms** has included the following Tenant's Property Tax Rebate Clause set forth below and in the FORMS section of this book.

TENANT'S PROPERTY TAX REBATE CLAUSE

Landlord agrees to provide a pro rata tax rebate to the tenant for each year in which the landlord receives a property tax reduction. Tenant's pro rata share of the property tax reduction shall be based upon the ratio which the number of square feet of tenant's dwelling bears to the total number of rentable square feet in the total building.

Landlord shall recoup all of the reasonable and necessary legal fees spent in obtaining the property tax rebate and shall only share with tenant the net amount of the property tax rebate after deducting such legal fees.

COST OF LIVING ALLOWANCES

At lease renewal time or annually if you have a lease stretching for a term of years, your landlord will want to increase the rent in order to cover his cost of living increases. These kinds of increases are abbreviated and called COLAS.

COLAS are based upon increases in the Consumer Price Index (the "CPI"). The CPI is published monthly by the Department of Labor of the Federal government as an index of inflation. The CPI tracks the average change in prices for all consumer goods. You can also use the CPI as an index of measurement in order to see how much the cost of living has risen in one year. As with any index it needs a base period in order to reflect increases from that base period time.

Also as with any index there is no assurance that there is any relationship between the CPI and the cost of housing.

When you negotiate a COLA with your landlord, you want to push the base period as far in the future as possible such as the month at the end of the first year of your lease not the month of the beginning of the lease.

COLAS should have a reasonable nexus with the geographical area in which you live. You don't want your rent increase tied to the inflation rate in Argentina or some banana republic. You want the cost of living tied to your local geographical area. After all, this is the area where you and your landlord live and spend your money.

OTHER LANDLORD INDEXES

Your landlord may want to tie his rent increases to indexes other than the CPI. The U.S. Department of Labor also maintains an index of landlord's operating costs. This index is much more accurate in reflecting increases in the landlord's true operating costs and comes much closer to protecting the landlord's bottom line income from inflation.

THE LANDLORD'S OPERATING COST INDEX IS NORMALLY HIGHER THAN THE CONSUMER PRICE INDEX AND WILL RESULT IN A LARGER RENT INCREASE TO YOU.

If you have the negotiating power, hold out for a rent increase tied to a percentage of your local CPI.

NO LESS FAVORABLE RENEWAL LEASE

When you are renewing your lease with your landlord, you don't want to have to start from square one and renegotiate every provision of your lease again. Assuming you have used **Lease On Your Terms** the first time and are reasonably happy with your lease, you don't want substantial renegotiations upon renewal.

Lease On Your Terms has incorporated an idea from the New York City rent stabilization law. This law and the clause we have adopted from it guarantees the tenant that the renewal lease must contain the same conditions as the expiring lease. Accordingly, the rights and privileges you have negotiated for under your old lease cannot be taken away by the landlord in the new lease.

In effect, the terms and conditions of the old lease favorable to the tenant must continue. The old lease clauses favorable to you cannot be deleted. They become what lawyers call the "law of the case" between the parties.

This is a fair rule when a contract is a living document between the parties and everyone is living under the contract. The same theory generally applies in labor negotiations and every provision of a collectively bargained labor contract is not renegotiated at renewal time. For example, if you had a right to keep a pet under the old lease, no one could reasonably expect you to have to kill the dog when you sign a new lease.

Lease On Your Terms has drafted the Tenant's No Less Favorable Lease Renewal Clause set forth below and in the FORMS section of this book. This clause has a hidden bonus if, as and when your dwelling gets sold and the new owner wants you to sign his onerous form of lease.

TENANT'S NO LESS FAVORABLE LEASE RENEWAL CLAUSE

Landlord agrees that any renewal lease with tenant will contain no less favorable terms and conditions than the terms and conditions of this lease except for changes in the rent.

ASSESSING CHANGED MARKET CONDITIONS

Unless rents in your local area are regulated by law such as the New York rent control and rent stabilization law, prevailing rents will be set by the general market. When your lease ends, your landlord will want to renegotiate the amount of the rent. As expected, the landlord wants the highest rent he can get and the tenant wants to pay as little rent as possible.

Fortunately, there is a general market defining and limiting everyone's rental price expectations. The market price for your dwelling may have gone up or down.

In order to assess the changed market conditions you should go back to the real estate section of your local newspapers and to the classified advertisements. You may also want to consult with a real estate broker familiar with the residential market.

Also consult with the network you have built up as a result of your last search for a dwelling. The network of friends and peers should furnish fast and reliable information as to existing rents and vacancies.

A quick refresher course in the now prevailing price levels in your general market should put you on equal bargaining footing with your landlord.

Your needs should also be evenly balanced. Even though you would have to foot the cost of moving from the premises, your landlord has the expense of carrying a vacancy and advertising for a replacement tenant.

Lease On Your Terms has incorporated a short cut to determining the general market rental for your dwelling. This short cut works where the landlord is a multi-unit landlord and the dwellings are substantially similar in appearance and location. The theory is that the landlord agrees to rent to you on a basis equal to the lowest rent he has charged during the last sixty days for a comparable unit in his complex. This formula will also work on a lowest rental per square foot basis.

Clauses such as this in international agreements or large corporate purchasing agreements are called "most favored nations clauses". In effect, the landlord is telling you that at renewal, I will rent to you on a most favored nations basis which is I will charge you the same rent that I gave to the tenant who negotiated the best deal with me during the last two months.

How do you know if the landlord is telling the truth? How do you police the most favored nations pricing? Normally, there are no secrets in the world. You will find out if the landlord cheated you with the passage of time. In that case, you will have a contractual right to a rent refund.

The Tenant's Most Favored Nations Clause is set forth below and in the FORMS section of this book.

TENANT'S MOST FAVORED NATIONS CLAUSE

Landlord agrees that the rent on renewal of this lease shall be no higher than the lowest rent charged by landlord to any other tenant in the building in which the premises is located for a comparable unit during the sixty days immediately preceding the expiry of this lease. This formula may be applied on the basis of rent per square foot in the building, if no comparable unit exists.

PART 7

MOVING OUT PROBLEMS

HOW YOUR LEASE TERMINATES

Basically your lease can come to an end in one of three ways.

1. You are evicted for failure to pay your rent.

2. The lease ends by its terms.

3. Your landlord seeks to evict you for your alleged substantial violation of your lease.

THE DIFFERENCE BETWEEN NON-PAYMENT AND HOLD OVER ACTIONS

Non-Payment Actions

Example number 1 above is an action for non-payment of rent. All the landlord wants is his rent paid. You can normally cure the non payment at any time until a warrant of eviction is signed by the judge by either paying the landlord or the clerk of the court in which the action is pending.

The discussion above relates to New York law. CHECK YOUR LOCAL STATE AND MUNICIPAL LAW TO FIND OUT HOW NON-PAYMENT ACTIONS WORK IN YOUR JURISDICTION.

Holdover Actions

In a holdover action the landlord does not want the rent; the landlord wants you out as a tenant. The landlord wants his dwelling back. You may want to remain but the landlord does not want you as a tenant. The term "holdover" derives from your holding over in the premises after the landlord had declared the lease at an end.

CONSEQUENCES OF YOUR BREAKING THE LEASE

In most states if you fail to honor a covenant (a fancy way of saying a promise) in a lease, the lease has been broken by you and comes to an end. The consequences of lease termination are flaming and dramatic. In theory and in fact, you could be evicted from your residence and also liable in money damages for monthly rent and legal fees until the landlord finds a replacement tenant.

NON-PAYMENT OF RENT

Non-payment of rent actions are normally just what the title suggests. The tenant has defaulted in the payment of rent and the landlord has brought an action to evict the tenant unless the tenant redeems the default. The case becomes much more complicated when the tenant has a defense or his own action against the landlord (called a counterclaim).

Under any set of circumstances it is good advice to get a lawyer when you are sued by the landlord for eviction. It is time to get a lawyer or legal advice whenever you are served with legal papers. You will need legal advice in order to defend yourself.

Often the reason the tenant has not paid the rent is because the landlord has failed to repair and maintain the dwelling and the common areas in the building. The tenant has a legitimate defense to the landlord's non-payment of rent action. All the more reason for the tenant to seek legal counsel. In this way the court can decide how to treat the larger issues of seeing that your monthly rent is used for the effective up keep of the rented premises.

Your lawyer will press all of your legal arguments to the court. In the end, (hopefully) Justice will prevail and (hopefully) a fair result reached by the court.

HOLDOVER ACTIONS

There are basically two kinds of holdover actions. One type of holdover occurs when the term of your lease ends. The second type of holdover occurs when your landlord has declared your lease to be terminated because you have committed an alleged substantial violation of the lease.

Expiry of the Term of Your Lease

Your lease has a definite term during which you have rented the premises. There is a provision in the lease which says that this lease commences on day 1 and ends on day 365. Your right to occupy the premises terminates on day 366 unless

1. you have renewed the lease,

2. you are protected by some local rent control law such as the New York City laws pertaining to rent control and rent stabilization.

Accordingly on and after day 366 you are a holdover tenant. Your status has diminished and you are at the mercy of your landlord (and the judges).

You should verify the law in your jurisdiction on this point. Unless the landlord has another tenant waiting for the dwelling, he will accept your rent checks in which event you will become a month to month tenant with a tenancy terminable upon 30 days notice. This means that the landlord must give you 30 days notice before he can evict you as a holdover. But once again check the law in your jurisdiction. The above summary is the New York rule.

Violation of Your Lease

Under New York law and hopefully the law of any civilized state, ONLY your SUBSTANTIAL violation of your lease will constitute grounds for the landlord to bring a holdover proceeding against you.

Substantial violation means a violation of real substance. In order to be a substantial violation the breach of the lease must be serious in nature and continuing in duration. You must have acted so despicably that you have antagonized your neighbors over and again or rendered damage of a substantial nature to the landlord's property.

The doctrine of substantial violation is where the bullet hits the bone. We are now discussing that balance where you want to enjoy the use and occupancy of your dwelling but your activities are treading on everyone else's desire to enjoy their use and occupancy of their dwellings.

This is also the area where your actions can cause harm or damage to your landlord or his property. For example, you cannot use your dwelling to manufacture explosives, run a bawdy house or deal drugs. Various laws affecting health and safety would cause such activities to be a substantial violation of your lease.

DEFENSES TO SUBSTANTIAL VIOLATION HOLDOVER ACTION

Suppose your landlord sues to evict you from your residence based upon your alleged substantial violation of any covenant in the lease or the rules and regulations of the landlord. IF YOU WANT TO CONTINUE LIVING THERE, YOU PROBABLY NEED A LAWYER.

There are defenses to a substantial proceeding. They range from the violation not being substantial to the landlord is barred from objecting because his super knew of the violation and the landlord accepted your rent check with knowledge of the breach. The rules may not have been agreed to by you or may be unreasonable. The landlord may have failed to warn you.

Just remember that you should consult with counsel whenever you receive a summons from your landlord.

Suppose You Give Notice of Termination

New York has a cute (for landlords) and oppressive (for tenants) law impacting on tenant's who give the landlord notice of the tenant's intention to quit the premises on a particular day.

In order to encourage tenants to move out on the specified day and otherwise lubricate the wheels of commerce the tenant who does not "deliver up" the premises must pay double rent to the landlord. Laws like this put the financial burden on the tenant to vacate. This type of law is designed to prevent the game of musical chairs. Remember what occurs when the landlord re-rents the premises to tenant number 2 effective on day 366 because you, as the tenant in possession, had expected to move out on day 365.

Just to protect you against laws like this, **Lease ON Your Terms** has added a Tenant's Holdover Clause set forth below and in the FORMS section of this book.

TENANT'S HOLDOVER CLAUSE

If tenant gives notice of his intention to quit the premises and does not deliver up possession at the time specified in such notice or otherwise becomes a holdover tenant, tenant shall continue to pay the same rent at the same time and in the same manner as otherwise payable hereunder so long as tenant shall continue in possession.

APPLICATION OF CLAUSES

The following clauses in this section shall apply regardless of how the lease terminated. It will make no difference whether the lease terminated for non-payment of rent or by a holdover proceeding.

MITIGATION OF DAMAGES

If a tenant moves out of a residence owing rent or otherwise breaks the contract of lease, the landlord who seeks damages is under the duty to mitigate those damages. Mitigate the damages means to take affirmative steps to lessen or reduce the damages. The landlord must try to reduce his damages by making a reasonable effort to relet the dwelling wrongfully vacated by the tenant.

This is know by lawyers as the duty to mitigate damages. Mitigate means to lessen. The landlord cannot just sit back and do nothing except collect rent from you for the duration of the lease. The landlord has to take all reasonable efforts to relet the residence.

The action the landlord must take to mitigate the damages is a matter of proof which will differ with the facts of each case.

The landlord's duty to mitigate damages is a defense to you if the landlord sues you for the unpaid rent. You will have to prove to the court that the landlord has not taken reasonable steps to rent the residence to another tenant.

Lease On Your Terms has a few tricks of its own and has a Tenant's Mitigation of Damages clause. Imagine a large apartment house or trailer park with three hundred fifty units and a vacancy rate of ten percent. This would mean that the landlord has 35 of his own units empty and available to rent. A ten percent vacancy factor is not unreasonable. Suppose you have vacated a unit and are still liable for monthly rent on that unit. When a new prospect comes to rent a unit, which unit do you think the landlord will show first? Will the landlord show a unit from inventory from which he derives no rent or will the landlord show the unit for which you are still liable for rent?

All those who voted that the landlord would show his own inventory unit first were right. In fact the landlord will fill all thirty four of his own units before trying to re-rent yours. Chances are by that time several of the landlord's other leases would have expired renewing his pot of unrented inventory units.

The law in most states is that the landlord can show his own unrented apartments prior to renting yours. **Lease ON Your Terms** has devised a clause compelling the landlord to use all reasonable efforts to re-rent your unit which will at least give you a right to stop paying the rent if you can prove that the landlord has made no attempt to rent your unit. Chances are, incidently, that the landlord will make no attempt to re-rent your unit as long as he thinks he will recover the rent from you.

How do you prove that the landlord had made no attempt to re-rent your unit? Revive that old straw person we used in the discrimination section in Part 1 of **Lease On Your Terms** to determine whether you have been discriminated against.

Send a straw person who approximates your landlord's ideal tenant to the landlord's office and try to rent a unit. Have the straw person keep a record of the units displayed by the landlord.

If your unit is shown, then you are getting a fair shake and have no complaint. If your unit is not shown, then you have a defense to the landlord's action against you for rent on the grounds that the landlord has failed to comply with his duty to mitigate damages under the law and under the Tenant' Mitigation of Damages cause of your lease.

In truth and in your negotiation posture with the landlord, each piece of real estate is unique. No two pieces of real estate in legal theory are the same. Each has a different view out the windows and a different physical location. Even in a hi-rise building, some tenants prefer high floors and some want low floors. And of course the views differ from each floor. Each unit also has different neighbors who may or may not have children, be more quiet than other neighbors and the like. Accordingly, the landlord should show your unit, even if it competes with his own unrented units. No one ever knows what will attract a prospective tenant.

The Tenant's Mitigation Of Damages Clause is set forth below and in the FORMS section of this book.

TENANT'S MITIGATION OF DAMAGES CLAUSE

Landlord agrees at the end of this lease to take all reasonable steps necessary to show tenant's premises to all new prospective tenants in order to mitigate tenant's liabilities hereunder.

TENANT'S RIGHT TO REMOVE FIXTURES AND IMPROVEMENTS

At common law any improvement to the premises reverted to the landlord at the end of the lease. This meant that anything you had affixed to the realty became property of the landlord. Bookcases, cabinets, outside TV antennas and the like are improvements of this nature. You don't want to discover that the Tiffany or crystal chandelier you hung in the dining room has reverted to the landlord.

This should not be a problem under 20th century leases. Generally, the landlord obligates the tenant to remove at tenant's expense all installations or attachments to the dwelling and restore and repair the premises to its original condition.

One strange and unexpected wrinkle at common law was that the tenant could lose the right to remove fixtures or improvements by reason of his acceptance of a new lease of the same premises without any surrender of possession between terms. This also should not be a problem today.

Just in case, however, **Lease On Your Terms** has included a clause authorizing the tenant to remove all fixtures and improvements.

The Tenant's Removal Of Fixtures and Improvements Clause is set forth below and in the FORMS section of this book.

TENANT'S REMOVAL OF FIXTURES AND IMPROVEMENTS CLAUSE

When this lease ends, Tenant may remove all fixtures, installations or attachments which tenant has placed at any time in or on the premises.

SELF-HELP EVICTION

Previously at common law virtually all leases provided that in case of a breach of the terms of the lease the landlord could remove the tenant "with or without legal process". This clause is an anachronism in the modern world. Self-help eviction should violate any civilized statute. **Lease On Your Terms** has not researched the changing laws of each state but has installed a tenant's clause that says that the landlord will not resort to self-help eviction. No one wants to come home and find a padlock on the door, the locks changed, and your personal property on the street in the rain.

The Tenant's No Self-Help Clause is set forth below and in the FORMS section of this book.

TENANT'S NO SELF-HELP CLAUSE

Landlord agrees not to resort to the remedy of self-help in the event of an alleged or purported breach of this lease by Tenant. It is the express understanding of the tenant and the landlord that all controversies arising from this lease be resolved by negotiation between the parties or by courts of competent jurisdiction.

DISTRAINT

Distraint at common law is the seizure of the tenant's property by a landlord to secure or satisfy payment of rent that is owed. Distraint is unlawful in certain states such as New Jersey. You have to check the law in your state and city to discover if the old common law doctrine of distraint applies.

You don't want the landlord holding your personal possessions as hostages for the payment of rent or damages under the lease. Besides you probably need your clothes, cooking utensils and furniture for general living purposes.

If the landlord objects to this clause, tell him that any disputes between landlord and tenant should be be resolved by a court and paid for in money damages. The landlord knows you are good for the money because otherwise you would have been rejected as a tenant. You just don't want your personal property tied up during the dispute resolving process. Besides, you may need your long underwear on a cold and windy day.

Lease On Your Terms does not favor distraint and has the landlord expressly waive any rights of distraint. The Tenant's No Distraint Clause is set forth below and in the FORMS section of this book.

TENANT'S NO DISTRAINT CLAUSE

Landlord hereby waives any right of distraint or other like remedy landlord may have at common law, by state or local law, or otherwise under this lease.

SECURITY INTERESTS

A security interest is a lien upon goods to satisfy an obligation. A bank lien on your car is an example of a security interest. Your car can be repossessed by the bank, if you fail to repay the bank loan.

Some landlords have a grant of a security interest in all of tenant's personal property given to the landlord as additional collateral for the payment of the tenant's obligations under the lease. This particular clause is absolutely insufferable and unconscionable. You don't want to come home one day to find that the landlord has changed the locks or sent all your personal property into storage at your expense pending sale for the landlord's benefit unless you pay the landlord's demands.

Lease On Your Terms has seen landlords take security interests in the tenant's goods. This appears to be a standard clause in the Pennsylvania form of lease. A basically fair and decent man like William Penn must be spinning in his grave.

The Tenant's No Security Interest Clause in the lease is set forth below and in the FORMS section of this book. It contains a provision that the landlord renounces any security interest in your goods which the landlord may have at law or in the lease.

TENANT'S NO SECURITY INTEREST CLAUSE

Landlord acknowledges that landlord takes no grant of a security interest in any of the tenant's personal property. Landlord hereby renounces any such security interest which landlord may otherwise have.

CONFESSIONS OF JUDGMENT

A confession of judgment means exactly what it says. The weaker party to the transaction agrees in advance of any dispute that the stronger party is so right that the court should enter an immediate judgment for the stronger party without even hearing the case.

Confessions of judgment are particularly distasteful clauses to the weaker party to a contract who is confessing that the stronger party be entitled to enter judgment prior to even notifying, charging or suing for the claim in question.

The party having the heft in bargaining power forces the weaker party to agree in advance that the stronger party is entitled to enter judgment immediately against the weaker party. Even if a genuine dispute arises under the contract, lease or note, the weaker party finds that he has already agreed in advance that the stronger party is correct and entitled to enter and enforce a legal judgment against the weaker person.

Lease On Your Terms says that civilization began when the strong gave up their right to eat the weak. In a civilized society you are pretty certain that you can walk the streets without someone stronger than you killing you for fresh meat. Confessions of judgment are very close to legal cannibalism.

They are outlawed in many states for consumer transactions. They are legal in some states in commercial transactions only after a breach of the contract has occurred and a settlement has been reached. Even in those states where they are legal,

confessions of judgment are a sign of immense distrust. It is difficult to deal with someone who is so afraid of the legal system that he doesn't even want to give you a day in court to defend yourself. After all, you may be right; you may have a defense or you may have a counterclaim against the holder of the confession of judgment.

Confessions of judgment appear to be used routinely in Pennsylvania.

Lease ON Your Terms advises against signing confessions of judgment unless you have a gun to your head, nowhere else to go, no other alternatives and no bargaining power.

Lease On Your Terms has included a Tenant's No Confession of Judgment Clause to be added as a rider to the lease. ONLY USE THIS CLAUSE IF THE LANDLORD HAS A CONFESSION OF JUDGMENT BUILT INTO HIS STANDARD FORM OF LEASE. THIS IS ONE OF THE CLAUSES THAT YOU NEED TO COUNTER THE LANDLORD'S PRE-PRINTED CLAUSE. IF THE LEASE DOES NOT HAVE A CONFESSION OF JUDGEMENT IN IT, KEEP YOUR POWDER DRY AND NEGOTIATE FOR SOMETHING ELSE YOU REALLY NEED.

The Tenant's No Confession of Judgment Clause is set forth below and in the FORMS section of this book.

TENANT'S NO CONFESSION OF JUDGMENT CLAUSE

Notwithstanding anything else to the contrary herein or elsewhere, this lease shall not be deemed to have any confessions of judgment in it in favor of any party. No party to this lease intends to or has confessed judgment on any matter relating to this lease.

EXEMPT PROPERTY

Under State law and the Federal Bankruptcy Act certain property of a debtor is exempt by law from levy and sale pursuant to a judgement creditor's execution. In plain English this means that certain property of a debtor cannot be touched by creditors. The type and amount of exempt property vary from state to state. It is beyond the purview of this book to report upon the exempt property laws of each state. Just to whet your appetite for your own pursuit of this area, in Florida, for example, a homestead is exempt property regardless of the size. In other states the property exempt may include a worker's tools, a gold wedding band, personal wardrobe and the like.

Some unscrupulous landlords have hidden clauses in the lease giving them a security interest (see above) or pledge of the tenant's personal property which is otherwise exempt by law from levy and sale by virtue of an execution. (This means property exempt from the reach of creditors.) The otherwise exempt then becomes security for the payment of rent due or to become due under the lease.

This clause is anathema and should give you an idea of the rapacity of your prospective landlord. It is an unreasonable clause and goes beyond all bounds of decency. What kind of "pond scum" landlord would want to take a woman's gold wedding band for unpaid rent?

Lease On Your Terms has a Tenant's Exempt Property Clause in which the landlord expressly waives and renounces any lease clauses granting landlord a security interest or pledge of tenant's property exempt by law from levy and sale by pursuant to an execution.

The Tenant's Exempt Property Clause is set forth below and in the FORMS section of this book.

TENANT'S EXEMPT PROPERTY CLAUSE

No security interest or pledge is granted by tenant to landlord of tenant's personal property exempt by law from levy and sale by virtue of an execution. Landlord expressly waives and renounces any clause in the printed lease contrary hereto.

PART 8

MOBILE HOME PARKS

The greatest abuses in residential leases probably occur in rentals of mobile home sites. The abuses fall into several generic categories resulting from the operator's failure to disclose the full nature of the transaction to the tenant.

Often the transaction is a sale of the mobile home to the tenant with the sales price structured as disguised payments of rent. The tenant is also forced to rent a plot of land on which to place the mobile home. This is usually the only true rental in the deal.

The problem occurs when the tenant wants to move the mobile home to a different location. The cost of moving the mobile home is prohibitive. It is normally cheaper to sell the mobile home and move into another mobile home park. The tenant then discovers that the only buyer for the mobile home is the operator of the old mobile home park and the depreciated purchase price is a fraction of the original price paid by the tenant-seller.

Eventually the true nature of the transaction appears. When the tenant tries to move into a new mobile home park, the new operator is only interested in selling the tenant a new mobile home at an inflated price and has no interest in moving the old mobile from the other location.

Before you move into a mobile home community check the reputation of the operator with the Attorney General's office of the state in which you live or with the Better Business Bureau. Obtain the address of your Better Business Bureau from your local telephone book.

For your convenience a form letter to the Better Business Bureau is set forth below and is contained in the FORMS Section of this book.

LETTER TO BETTER BUSINESS BUREAU

Better Business Bureau

_____
Insert street address

_____
Insert city, state and zip code

_____
Insert date

RE: PURCHASE OF MOBILE HOME OR HOMESITE

Gentlemen:

I am currently considering a purchase of a mobile home or lease of a mobile homesite from the dealer or business set forth below:

_____
Insert name of business

_____
Insert street address of business

_____
Insert city, state and zip code

Would you please advise as to whether there are any complaints on file with your organization against that vendor.

Very truly yours,

_____
Insert your name

_____
Insert your street address

_____
Insert your city, state, and zip code

Since mobile home sales generally involve people somewhat lower on the income and educational scales than more expensive housing, the area is ripe for undiscovered fraud and abuse.

Mobile homes may appear to be the most affordable form of housing in the short run. You must check for the undiscovered loopholes that could cost more in the long run. The cheapest housing available may actually cost more.

Most importantly, you must ascertain the availability and cost of the lifeline hookups for sewer, water, electricity, gas and telephone.

Lease On Your Terms believes that as a general rule all of the provisions of this book relating to other forms of dwellings also apply with equal vigor to mobile homes and mobile home parks. Don't be put off by anyone. YOU SHOULD CHECK THE LOCAL LAW OF YOUR STATE AND MUNICIPALITY IN ORDER TO BE CERTAIN.

You should have the same rights to use and enjoy your mobile home that any movie star has when renting a beach front home in Malibu, California. These rights would also apply to the use of a reasonable garden plot around the mobile home.

Just be certain of the right to move your home and the costs of moving that home to a new homesite.

PART 9

YOUR TENANT'S MISCELLANEOUS LEGAL CHANGES TO BE ADDED AS RIDERS TO THE LANDLORD'S STANDARD LEASE

Most of the clauses we will be discussing in this Part are the boring technical clauses in the lease which are normally referred to by lawyers as the "boiler plate." "Boiler plate" as best as can be determined by the author refers to the days when legal forms and documents were manually set by printers in metal linotype which looked like the metal from melted down boilers.

But don't be fooled. What some call normal "boiler plate" others call important substantive legal rights. Great legal benefit and harm is buried in the long gray lines of print that no one really wants to read.

Lease On Your Terms will defuse the harm in the "boiler plate" by explaining what the major clauses mean so that you can make informed choices as to what decisions you wish to make.

DEFINITIONS CLAUSE

Your tenant's riders refer to the person owning the real estate as the "landlord" and the person(s) renting the real estate as the "tenant".

The original draft of the standard lease used by the landlord may refer to him as the "lessor", the "owner", the somewhat archaic "party of the first part" or any of a dozen other words or phrases. You may be referred to in the original draft as the "lessee", the "renter" or the "party of the second part".

It really doesn't matter what you are called or how you are defined or designated in the original draft of the lease so long as you know who you are and can read and understand the provisions of the lease.

You will note that **Lease On Your Terms** has pre-printed rip out riders that you can detach from this book and present to your landlord during the course of negotiations. Since our riders are pre-printed, the definitional terms "landlord" and "tenant" used in your riders may not intermesh with the definitional terms in the body of the landlord's original form of standard residential lease. Accordingly the Tenant's Definitions Clause will harmonize the terms by stating that regardless of the definitions in the main body of the lease the riders will refer to the person owning the real estate as the "landlord" and to the person(s) leasing the real estate as the "tenant." We believe this not only coincides with colloquial usage but also reflects economic reality.

The Tenant's Definitions Clause is set forth below and in the FORMS section of this book.

TENANT'S DEFINITIONS CLAUSE

For purposes of these riders _____

                             Insert name(s) of tenant(s)

shall be referred to individually and collectively as the "tenant",

         and _____

                    Insert name of landlord

shall be referred to as the "landlord".

These definitional terms of tenant and landlord shall be deemed to mesh and be read in context with whatever definitional terms each party may have in the main body of the lease.

RIDER INCLUSION CLAUSE

You need a tie-in clause to tie your riders to the lease. The clause set forth below and in the FORMS section of this book will add your tenant's riders to the lease with the same force and effect as if they were contained in the landlord's original form of lease.

YOU WILL ALWAYS NEED THIS CLAUSE AS A BRIDGE BETWEEN THE MAIN TEXT OF THE LANDLORD'S LEASE AND THE INCLUSION OF YOUR RIDERS.

The Tenant's Rider Inclusion Clause is set forth below and in the FORMS section of this book.

TENANT'S RIDER INCLUSION CLAUSE

It is agreed between the landlord and the tenant that the Tenant's Riders to this lease be and hereby are deemed to be part of this lease with the same force and effect as if set forth in their entirety in the pre-printed body of the lease.

SUPREMACY CLAUSE

You are using your tenant's riders to detoxify the landlord's poison pen clauses in the landlord's pre-printed standard form of lease. What happens when your clause conflicts with the landlord's clause? How does a judge know how to interpret the intent of the parties when he resolves the battle of the clauses?

The answer is the Tenant's Supremacy Clause set forth below and in the FORMS section of this book. The Tenant's Supremacy Clause tells the judge that your clause reigns in the battle of the clauses.

TENANT'S SUPREMACY CLAUSE

The riders to this lease shall be deemed to supplement the original text of the landlord's form of lease when both clauses are in agreement.

In the case of conflict the terms of the riders shall be deemed to override and supersede the terms of the original landlord's form of lease. The intent of the parties to this lease is that the tenant has bargained for and otherwise paid for the inclusion of these riders and should receive the benefit of the rights contained in the riders to this lease.

WARRANTY OF HABITABILITY

The warranty of habitability is not part of the boiler plate. This clause is on the leading edge of tenants' rights. In simple terms a warranty of habitability means that the landlord has to keep the residence and public areas up to standard living conditions. The theory is that the landlord guarantees that the residence and common areas are fit for human habitation and that there will be no conditions which will be detrimental to life, health or safety.

In other words your expectations when you rent a dwelling are that the dwelling is suitable to live in. If you wanted to live in a cave without electricity, security, heat and running water, you would be living in the great outdoors by choice. You don't expect to rent a dwelling and then discover that the landlord fails to make all necessary repairs and maintenance to keep the dwelling habitable, safe and livable.

In exchange for your rent payments, you have every right to expect the landlord to guarantee that the residence is fit to live in and will continue to be fit to live in. If the landlord does not maintain and repair the premises, your expectations have been shattered and the value of the residence to you has been diminished.

The concept is that of a warranty of habitability. A warranty is a form of guarantee that goes to the heart of a transaction. Under this concept the landlord is promising to guarantee that your rented dwelling is and will be fit for habitation and that the landlord will make all repairs necessary to maintain the premises as liveable.

If the landlord fails to make all necessary repairs, you will have certain rights including the right to stop paying rent or to make the repairs and deduct the cost of the repairs from the rent. You could also defend a non-payment of rent or eviction action by the landlord against you by demonstrating to the court that the landlord has breached his promise of the guarantee of habitability to you.

Under New York and New Jersey law an express warranty of habitability exists. The concept has also been applied in the District of Columbia, New Hampshire, Hawaii and Wisconsin.

In some jurisdictions there is an implied warranty of habitability. An implied warranty is read into the lease under the theory that the landlord has to deliver suitable living conditions as well as occupancy of the rented premises.

The way to get judges in your jurisdiction to accept the concept of a warranty of habitability is to check your local building code or housing code or housing maintenance code. Obviously, these building, maintenance and housing codes were designed to protect people like you. You are a third party beneficiary of the provisions of those codes. The codes were not just designed to allow the local authorities to control building construction and landlord's actions.

The codes were written for your benefit.

For these reasons your local judge should read the building, maintenance and housing codes into your lease with the same force and effect as if they had been set forth in your lease in their entirety. After all, those building, maintenance and housing standards read as a whole is what habitability is all about. The law has already defined habitability in those codes and the landlord has to comply with the law. The landlord's warranty of habitability merely gets the landlord to agree that he will comply with the existing law.

Lease On Your Terms has an express warranty of habitability as a clause to be negotiated by you. This will protect tenants who live in states with no warranty of habitability. The local building code and housing maintenance code should not be regulated by some board of fat, lazy, uncaring bureaucrats. It should be policed by caring citizens who are directly concerned with enforcement of those rules. You are in a much better position to discover code violations and to remedy the situation in private redress. All the state or city can usually do is to fine the landlord who has breached the codes. You can deduct the cost of repairs from your rent.

The warranty of habitability ties in with the question of necessary repairs.

In most states the tenant may raise the breach of habitability as a defense and set-off in an action brought by the landlord for non-payment of rent. The tenant can show that he is entitled to a rent abatement for landlord's breach of an implied or express warranty of habitability. If the tenant is successful, he need not pay the full rent but only the reasonable value of the premises in its imperfect condition. The Tenant may also get a court order allowing the tenant to deduct the cost of repairs to a vital facility from the rent otherwise payable.

If the tenant is unsuccessful, he must pay the full amount of the rent and court costs immediately or he will be evicted.

As a prerequisite to maintaining a successful rent rebate action, the tenant must comply with certain reasonable ground rules. First, the tenant must give the landlord positive, reasonable and seasonable notice of the alleged defect. Second, the tenant must request its correction and must allow the landlord a reasonable period of time to effect the repair or replacement. Not every defect or inconvenience will be deemed to constitute a breach of the covenant of habitability. The condition complained of must be such as truly to render the premises uninhabitable in the eyes of a reasonable person.

The following criteria are suggestive and not exhaustive. They are worthy of consideration in determining whether or not there has been a breach of the covenant of habitability on the part of the landlord.

1. Have housing codes, building codes or sanitary regulations been violated?

2. Does the defect or deficiency affect a vital facility?

3. Does the defect or deficiency effect safety and sanitation?

4. How long has it existed?

5. How old is the structure?

6. Is the tenant responsible?

7. Has the tenant waived the defect or be precluded from complaining?

The Tenant's Warranty of Habitability Clause is set forth below and in the FORMS section of this book.

TENANT'S WARRANTY OF HABITABILITY CLAUSE

All of the sections of this lease are subject to the provisions of a warranty of habitability expressly made by landlord to tenant. Nothing in this lease shall be interpreted to mean that tenant has waived any rights concerning the warranty of habitability. Landlord agrees that the residence and the common areas are fit for human habitation and that there are no conditions which are or will be suffered to be detrimental to life, health or safety.

TENANT'S LEGAL FEES

Leases always provide for the tenant to pay the landlord's legal fees and disbursements in any law suit arising from tenant's default under the lease or for defending lawsuits brought against the landlord by the tenant.

Leases almost never have a clause requiring the landlord to pay the tenant's legal fees in the event the tenant prevails. New York State has an implied covenant of reciprocity with regard to attorney's fees. Under this implied covenant the landlord is required to pay the victorious tenant's legal fees, if the lease requires the tenant to pay the landlord's legal fees.

Under the New York law you have the right to collect from the landlord reasonable legal fees and expenses incurred in a successful defense by you of a lawsuit brought by the landlord against you or brought by you against the landlord, if the lease obliges you to pay the landlord's legal fees. In other words, a Mexican stand-off exists in which the loser of the court case pays the legal fees of the winner.

Lease On Your Terms accepts the New York law as a reasonable compromise and has inserted a Tenant's Legal Fees Clause in this book.

The other problem is limiting your liability to reasonable and actual attorney's fees of the landlord. Under the landlord's standard form of lease, you are liable for all of the landlord's legal fees without regard as to whether the legal fees are reasonable or outrageous. You should only be responsible for reasonable attorney's fees charged by reasonable attorneys.

LEASE ON YOUR TERMS LIMITS YOUR RESPONSIBILITY TO THE LANDLORD'S REASONABLE ATTORNEY'S FEES. You don't want to find out after the case is over that the landlord's lawyer is his brother-in-law, Whiplash Willy, who has no other cases and devotes one hundred percent of his time to this case.

The Tenant's Legal Fees Clause is set forth below and in the FORMS section of this book.

TENANT'S LEGAL FEES CLAUSE

If either party to this lease shall bring any cause of action or proceeding against the other party for enforcement of this lease, the prevailing party shall recover reasonable and necessary legal fees and expenses from the loosing party.

WAIVER OF TRIAL BY JURY

Most standard lease forms force you to give up your right to a jury trial on any matters concerning (i) the lease, (ii) the relationship between you and your landlord and (iii) your use and occupancy of the rented premises.

The waiver of jury trial should not include claims for personal injury or property damage arising from negligence claims you may bring against the landlord.

Landlords know that everybody hates a landlord. Landlords feel more secure with a trial before a judge than a trial by jury. Juries know how sincerely outrageous and unreasonable landlords can be.

As a practical matter, you probably don't really care whether you have a trial by jury or a trial by a judge. The end result is usually the same. In a famous study of the efficacy of the jury system the University of Chicago conducted an extensive investigation of jury verdicts. They matched the jury verdict with the verdict the judge would have rendered and discovered no discernable difference.

After years of testing, the University of Chicago came to the conclusion that the jury system works well. A corollary conclusion was that the jury system worked well because juries rendered the same verdict as the judge, who presumably understood the rules of evidence and the weight to be accorded to each piece of evidence.

There was one aberrational case, however, in the jury study. One all women jury in Peoria, Illinois was deliberating on a case involving a woman who had lost both legs in an accident involving a train. It was a clear case of neglect on the railroad's part and the only issue was the amount of damages to be awarded to the plaintiff.

The railroad had already offered a settlement of several hundred thousand dollars to the plaintiff. This huge offer of payment was not communicated to the jury. The jury returned a verdict of $3600. This is not the old joke that the plaintiff didn't have a leg to stand on.

In a poll of the jury conducted by the University of Chicago Law School, one of the women on the jury claimed that the judge told the jury to make the award. When the judge charged the jury he directed them, "If you find that the railroad was negligent and is at fault, then you must compensate the plaintiff for her injuries."

The twelve women on the jury returned a verdict of $3600. There were 12 people on the jury and they each wrote out a personal check to the plaintiff for $300 (which was all they could afford).

"It's a terrible system," one woman of the jury told the University of Chicago investigator (who was the author's professor in law school), "but it's the American system so it must be right."

Unless you live in Peoria, **Lease On Your Terms** doesn't believe you lose much by giving up your right to a jury trial. Most of the time the facts will speak for themselves and be interpreted with substantially the same result by a judge or jury.

Furthermore, the legal system isn't geared to handle the shear volume of jury trials that landlord and tenant litigation would generate. A judge trial is quicker than the act of picking a jury. You wouldn't want to wait around and lose time from work while a jury is selected or deliberates.

For those readers who don't want to waive a jury trial and who feel that they have the negotiating heft to enforce that position, **Lease On Your Terms** has drafted a clause compelling a trial by jury. We suggest that you negotiate this clause like Marlon Brando's Godfather. Suggest that you want the right to a jury trial. Don't insist.

The Tenant's Right to a Jury Trial Clause is set forth below and in the FORMS section of this book.

TENANT'S RIGHT TO A JURY TRIAL CLAUSE

Nothing contained in this lease or otherwise shall constitute a waiver of the right to a trial by jury in a court action, proceeding or counterclaim on any matters concerning this lease, the relationship of the parties as landlord and tenant, or the tenant's use and occupancy of the dwelling.

WAIVER OF COUNTERCLAIM

The standard lease also wants you to give up your right to counterclaim against the landlord, if the landlord sues you for rent. The landlord's theory is that rent is the glue which binds the concrete of western civilization. If you could deduct what you claim the landlord owes you from your rent, the landlord could never meet his mortgage obligations. Accordingly, the landlord wants you to prosecute a separate action against the landlord instead of counterclaiming against the landlord when he sues you for rent.

Lease On Your Terms suggests that you abide by the landlord's clause under which you waive your right to counterclaim against the landlord. This clause is like the landlord's security blanket. He affectionately refers to the clause obligating you to pay your rent each month as the "Hell Or High Water Clause". He expects you to pay your rent come hell or high water.

After reading **Lease On Your Terms** you know that you can take reasonable actions to protect yourself and your family from harm. If the landlord fails to perform his duties and responsibilities and sues, you will get a day in court to explain the entire affair to a judge. The case usually involves the landlord failing to make repairs and the tenant withholding rent or applying rent to the repairs. The judge will listen to your side of the story.

Don't get too excited by the waiver of counterclaim. Normally you can bring up most matters by way of defense to the landlord's claim against you so the waiver of counterclaim doesn't generally matter a hill of beans.

GRACE PERIOD

A grace period is a period of time which the tenant will have to cure any default under the lease. Suppose you have been on vacation or in the hospital on the day your rent was due. You don't want the lease to come to a crashing end just because you were out of the country or in the hospital. A grace period gives you the chance to cure the default.

Lease On Your Terms has drafted a clause containing a seven business day period during which you can cure any default after landlord's written notice of default to you. The business days are necessary rather than calendar days because it is hard to transfer money on weekends and holidays.

The Tenant's Grace Period Clause is set forth below and in the FORMS section of this book.

TENANT'S GRACE PERIOD CLAUSE

Tenant shall have a seven business day grace period in which to cure any default under this lease. The seven day grace period shall commence upon the day that the landlord delivers written notice to the tenant of the alleged default.

EXCULPATORY CLAUSES LIMITING THE LANDLORD'S LIABILITY

In the past leases used to provide that a landlord may not be held liable for any injury or damages suffered by a tenant even though the injury was caused by the negligence of the landlord. Another strategy used by landlords is to limit their liability only to cases of "gross or wanton" negligence.

Today, in most civilized states provisions such as these have been declared to be against public policy and unenforceable.

Lease On Your Terms has not checked the law in each state. We can tell you that in New Jersey, for example, such clauses are invalid. **Lease On Your Terms** has addressed this problem by inserting a clause in the lease that specifically states that any clause by which the landlord attempts to limit his liability under law shall be null and void.

The Tenant's Exculpatory Clauses Shall Be Deemed Void Clause is set forth below and in the FORMS section of this book.

EXCULPATORY CLAUSES SHALL BE DEEMED VOID

Landlord and tenant agree that any clause in this lease attempting to exculpate the landlord from landlord's own negligence or misconduct shall be deemed null and void.

GUARANTY

Standard leases have a guaranty attached to the end of them. The guaranty generally provides for a second person guarantor to guarantee to the landlord the strict performance of and observance by Tenant of all the agreements, provisions and rules in the attached lease. The guaranty goes on to waive notice and the guarantor generally agrees to be equally liable with the tenant so that the landlord need not sue the tenant at all. Furthermore, the guaranty remains in full effect even if the lease is renewed.

The guarantor is a kind of co-signer for you. It means that the landlord doesn't quite trust in your financial responsibility. The landlord wants to look to a second person who will pay, if you don't.

Whether or not you provide a guarantor for your landlord is a matter of negotiation. Don't provide a guarantor unless you absolutely must.

Never sign a guaranty unless you intend to be fully responsible for the debt of another person. Don't be a fool with a fountain pen.

LIQUIDATED DAMAGES

Liquidated damages is a dollar amount of damages that the parties may agree in advance will represent the total damages a party will suffer from a broken contact. Needless to say, a lease is a contract.

You are more likely to be the person who breaches the lease. All the landlord has agreed to in the lease is to give you occupancy of the premises (and perhaps to keep the premises in good repair). You have the major burdens under the lease of paying rent each month and moving out at the expiration of the term of the lease.

If possible, you would like to put a dollar limit on your liability under the lease. You would like to place a cap on your liability. Even under the worst situation scenario, the dollar amount of your liability has been fixed by that ceiling. And you would also like to fix that amount as low as possible. No one likes to be liable to infinity which by definition is the largest number you can think of plus 1.

The types of damage you could cause the landlord could include (i) lost rent, (ii) physical damage to the premises and (iii) legal fees and costs of evicting you. Each of these components of damages will be discussed below to see if they can reasonably be liquidated.

Lost Rent

You and your landlord can quantify the amount of rent due under the lease by multiplying the monthly rent by the number of months in the lease. You and your landlord can also assess the general market conditions and guesstimate the number of months it will take to find a replacement tenant.

Accordingly, it may be possible for you and your landlord to agree that the landlord's damages for lost rent would be limited to a specific dollar amount or a certain number of month's rent. This would appear to be an item subject to negotiation.

Physical Damage to the Premises

It will be very difficult for you to get the landlord to agree to limit your damages for your physical damage to his premises. After all the amount of physical damage to the premises is within your direct control. You should be treating the landlord's property with the same care you devote to safeguarding your own property, reasonable wear and tear excepted.

You have fire and casualty insurance to protect you from damage beyond your control to the landlord's property.

In the final analysis you don't have to worry about the landlord damaging his own property and trying to holding you accountable. You have already prepared the detailed checklists from **Lease On Your Terms** which will be your safest shield.

Based upon this reasoning, you don't really need a limit on your liability for physical damages to the landlord's property and can live very well without it. In any event, your security deposit should cover routine cleaning and the like even if leave the place a tad littered.

Legal Fees and Costs of Eviction

This should be the easiest to agree upon with your landlord. We are talking about a negotiated settlement under which you hand your landlord the keys and a specific sum of money and he hands you a release. YOUR LANDLORD WILL HAVE NO LEGAL FEES OR COSTS OF EVICTION.

The Tenant's Liquidated Damages Clause is set forth below and in the FORMS section of this book.

TENANT'S LIQUIDATED DAMAGES CLAUSE

Landlord agrees that tenant's damages hereunder for unpaid rent shall be limited to $_____.
Nothing herein shall limit tenant's liability for:

    (i) physical damage to the premises or

    (ii) for reimbursement of landlord's reasonable and actual legal fees and expenses.

Insert amount

RELEASE

A release is a formal document under which parties to a deal, conflict or litigation end a transaction pursuant to a settlement agreement which is acceptable to each of them.

As it suggests the release is a release of all claims arising from certain defined transactions that each had against the other from the beginning of time until the signing of the release .

The form of release set forth in **Lease On Your Terms** is a mutual release. You and your landlord are releasing each other from all claims each has against the other under the lease. The terms of the release are limited to claims arising from your lease. It will not affect a claim for personal injury you may have pending against your landlord. But you should check with your personal injury lawyer just in case.

The Tenant's Release Form is set forth below and in the FORMS section of this book.

TENANT'S RELEASE FORM

In consideration of the sum of ten dollars and other good and valuable consideration the receipt of which is hereby acknowledged, the undersigned landlord and tenant hereby release each other from any and all claims that each had or may have had against the other arising from a certain lease between them.

_____
Insert name of landlord

_____
Insert name of tenant

_____
Insert date

Sworn to before me this

_____ day of _____, 199__

_____
Notary Public

_____
Seal.

PART 10

THE FORMS

Each of the riders previously discussed in **Lease On Your Terms** is pre-printed on the following perforated pages. Each individual rider that you desire to incorporate into the lease can be removed from this book and presented to your landlord as your proposed changes to the standard form of lease offered by your landlord.

Remember that you don't need every rider. **Lease On Your Terms** has helped you to understand your landlord's lease and why he feels he needs each clause. **Lease On Your Terms** has also shown why you may need relief from certain of the landlord's clauses.

The riders you need for your own protection will depend upon your own individual circumstances. Will you be moving before the lease terminates by the passage of time? How easy or difficult will finding a replacement tenant be? How tight or loose is your rental market? Is IBM or your town's largest employer hiring or firing? Only you know what riders and changes you need.

Use your common sense and the negotiating skills you have learned in this book to tailor make your own individualized self fulling lease arrangement with your landlord.

THE FORMS AND TENANT'S CLAUSES ARE SET FORTH IN THE FORMS SECTION IN THE SAME ORDER THAT THEY ARE FOUND IN THE BODY OF **LEASE ON YOUR TERMS**. THIS WAY THE FORMS AND CLAUSES BASICALLY FOLLOW THE FLOW OF THE LEASE TRANSACTION. THE FIRST THINGS YOU DO WILL BE FOUND IN THE EARLY FORMS AND SO ON.

IDENTITY OF NEW OCCUPANT FORM

Insert Date

Re: Notification of New Occupant

Insert name of Landlord

Insert landlord's street address

Insert landlord's city, state and zip code

Dear Landlord:

Reference is made to the lease between you and the undersigned for the premises set forth below. Please be advised that the person(s) listed below will be additional occupants of the premises rented from you by the undersigned.

NAME(S) OF ADDITIONAL OCCUPANT(S)

Very truly yours,

Insert your name(s) as on the lease

Insert your street address

Insert your City, State and Zip Code

IMPORTANT NOTE: BE CERTAIN THAT YOU ARE AUTHORIZED AN ADDITIONAL OCCUPANT BEFORE YOU SEND THIS NOTICE TO THE LANDLORD. REREAD THE ABOVE SECTION OF **LEASE ON YOUR TERMS** CONCERNING HOW MANY PEOPLE CAN LIVE IN ONE DWELLING.

TENANT'S NO BROKER CLAUSE

Landlord and tenant represent, warrant and covenant to each other that no broker brought about this lease. Landlord and tenant each indemnify and hold each other harmless from claims by any broker concerning this lease.

TENANT'S BROKER CLAUSE

Landlord and tenant represent, warrant and covenant to each other that no broker brought about this lease except for_____

_____
      Insert name and address of broker

_____.

It is agreed between the parties that the broker's fee will be paid by landlord (tenant). The amount of the broker's commission is $_____
                                  Insert amount

The broker's commission will be paid at the time and in the manner set forth below (Insert the time and manner of payment, i.e. cash or check at signing, in twelve equal payments on the first day of each month, etc.):

_____

_____

_____

_____

_____

BUDGET FORM

INCOME

After tax take home salary . . . . _____
Interest income . . . . _____
Dividend income . . . . _____
Alimony . . . . _____
Other . . . . _____
Other . . . . _____
Other . . . . _____
Other . . . . _____

Total . . . . _____

Next let's list your continuing and extraordinary expenses.

EXPENSES

Food . . . . _____
Current rent . . . . _____
Auto notes . . . . _____
Auto operating expense . . . . _____
Commuting to work . . . . _____
Clothes . . . . _____
Entertainment . . . . _____
Miscellaneous . . . . _____
Loan repayments . . . . _____
Alimony . . . . _____
Other . . . . _____
Other . . . . _____
Other . . . . _____
Other . . . . _____
Other . . . . _____

Total . . . . _____

COSTING OUT THE RENT FORM

Utilities . . . . ._____

Electric . . . . ._____

Gas . . . . ._____

Water . . . . ._____

Telephone . . . . ._____

Garbage removal . . . . ._____

Sewer . . . . ._____

Cable TV . . . . ._____

Master TV antenna charges . . . . ._____

Parking . . . . ._____

Laundry . . . . ._____

Air Conditioning costs . . . . ._____

Amenities (health club, pool, etc.) . . . . ._____

Storage space . . . . ._____

Other . . . . ._____

Other . . . . ._____

Other . . . . ._____

Other . . . . ._____

Total . . . . ._____

RECEIPT

RECEIVED ON THE DAY SET FORTH BELOW

FROM _____

           Insert your name

THE SUM OF $_____

           Insert the dollar amount

AS AND FOR A_____.

           Insert the reason for the payment, i.e., down payment,
                  advance payment of rent, etc.

THIS MONEY IS (IS NOT) REFUNDABLE UNDER THE FOLLOWING

CONDITIONS: _____

           Insert the conditions concerning a refund

_____

_____

_____

               _____
               Signature

               _____
               Title, i.e., manager, agent,
               Superintendent, landlord

               _____
               Street Address

               _____
               City, State and Zip Code

               _____
               Telephone number

               _____
               Form of identification

               _____
               Insert date

PROPERTY VIEWING AND KEYS AGREEMENT

I hereby acknowledge receipt of the key(s) to the dwelling at

_____.

I shall use the key(s) for the express purpose of viewing the dwelling in order to determine whether it is suitable for rental by me.

I have given the landlord or his agent a key deposit of $_____ receipt of which is hereby acknowledged. The key deposit shall be returned to me when I return the key(s).

I shall return the key(s) by_____(a.m.) (p.m.) today to the landlord or his agent at the same place where I received the key(s). Should I fail to return the key(s), the landlord is entitled to retain my deposit to pay for the cost of changing the locks on the dwelling.

_____
Insert your name Prospective Tenant

_____
Insert your street address

_____
Insert your city, state and zip code

_____
Insert your telephone reach number

_____
Insert date

RECEIPT OF ABOVE DEPOSIT ACKNOWLEDGED

_____
Landlord or agent.

RECORD OF VIEWING CHECKLIST

ADDRESS _____
_____
_____

TYPE OF BUILDING_____
(garden apartment, brownstone, hi-rise, home,
luxury, loft, etc.)

NUMBER OF ROOMS _____

TYPE OF
ROOMS_____
_____
_____
_____

MONTHLY RENT $_____

NUMBER OF MONTH'S ADVANCE RENT _____

SECURITY DEPOSIT $_____

TYPE OF
KITCHEN_____
AIR CONDITIONING_____

APPLIANCES_____

SQUARE FEET OF LIVING SPACE_____

PARKING_____

ESTIMATED COST OF UTILITIES_____
_____

AMENITIES_____
_____
_____
_____

SECURITY &
DOORMAN_____

LAUNDRY_____

PROXIMITY TO
SHOPPING_____
_____
_____

SCHOOL
DISTRICT_____

COMMUTE TO
WORK_____

_____

_____

CABLE TV_____

STORAGE BINS_____

TOTAL COST PER MONTH:

Rent . . . . ._____
Utilities . . . . ._____
Parking . . . . ._____
Cable TV . . . . ._____
Amenities . . . . ._____
Laundry . . . . ._____
Storage bins . . . . . . ._____
Other . . . . ._____
Other . . . . ._____
Other . . . . ._____
Other . . . . ._____
Other . . . . ._____
Other . . . . ._____

TOTAL COS . . . . ._____

WHAT DID YOU LIKE ABOUT THIS AS A RESIDENCE?

_____
_____
_____
_____
_____
_____
_____
_____
_____

WHAT DID YOU DISLIKE ABOUT THIS AS A RESIDENCE?

_____
_____
_____
_____
_____
_____
_____
_____
_____

OVER-ALL RATING_____

TENANT'S ORAL REPRESENTATION CLAUSE

This lease constitutes the full agreement between the parties and there have been no oral representations made except for the following oral representations made by the landlord:

Insert landlord's oral representations:

1.

2.

3.

4.

CREDIT VERIFICATION AND REFUND AGREEMENT FORM

RECEIVED FROM_____
Insert your name

as a prospective tenant the sum of $_____
Insert amount

to be used solely for the purpose of requesting a Consumer Report under the Federal Fair Credit

Reporting Act and otherwise verifying the information submitted on an application to rent premises

situate at and commonly known as_____
Insert street, city and state address

_____.

This sum is to be refunded if (i) the landlord or his agent ("landlord") selects another tenant to re

nt the dwelling prior to requesting the Consumer Report or (ii) a lease is signed between landl

ord and this prospective tenant.

_____
Landlord or agent

_____
Prospective tenant

_____
Date

_____
Time

TENANT'S DEPOSIT AGREEMENT FORM

Landlord hereby acknowledges receipt of the sum of $ _____

Insert amount of deposit

received from _____

Insert name of tenant(s)

(hereinafter referred to as the "prospective tenant(s)") to be held by landlord as a
totally refundable deposit for the purpose of holding premises situate and known as
(Insert unit number, street, city and state address and zip code):

_____

_____

_____

until _____

Insert date when reservation of unit terminates

or until the landlord verifies prospective tenant(s)' rental application.

This deposit shall be totally refundable to the prospective tenant(s) whether or not the prospective
tenant shall rent the premises.

_____
Landlord

_____
Prospective Tenant(s)

_____
Prospective Tenant(s)

_____
Date

116

CHECK LIST

PREMISES SITUATED AT

_____

_____

_____

This checklist was made by the tenant(s) prior to moving into the above stated premises. All notes reflected in this checklist were made contemporaneously with the an examination of the premises by the tenant(s) and the landlord or witness.

This checklist is made to serve as a business record of the events recorded herein, namely the condition of the premises prior to the date the tenant(s) took possession of the premises.

The landlord or his agent have been invited to join in the preparation of this check list and have (have not) participated.

_____
Tenant(s)

_____
Witness

_____
Landlord

_____
Date

CHECK LIST

ENTRY ROOM
Ceiling and Walls—describe any holes. State size and depth in inches or millimeters.

_____

_____

Describe any cracks and the length of each._____

_____

_____

Falling plaster_____

_____

Peeling paint_____

_____

Look for discolored yellow or brown marks indicating water leaks
from the floor above and describe them._____

_____

_____

_____

Floor—describe any holes and the size and depth of each in inches or
millimeters._____

_____

_____

Note any soft spots where floor gives when stepped on.

_____

_____

_____

Note any significant degree of slant._____

_____

_____

Note any ripped or cracked linoleum or floor covering._____

_____

_____

Windows—Inspect glass closely.
Note any cracks, holes, or missing glass._____

_____

_____

_____

Check window panes for loose putty and note if panes are loose in the
mullions._____

_____

_____

_____

Open windows and note if they slide up and down._____

_____

_____

_____

Note whether windows stay in raised position without falling.

_____

_____

_____

Inspect screens and storms for serviceability and note rips, cracks and tears etc._____

_____

_____

_____

Note whether there is a lock on the window and does it work?_____

_____

_____

_____

Is there a fire escape and how secure is it for escape and to keep out intruders?_____

_____

_____

_____

Check windows for drafts._____

_____

_____

Electrical—Count the number of electrical outlets. Verify and note whether they work._____

_____

_____

Do all light switches work?_____

_____

_____

Is there unwrapped and exposed wiring in contravention of building codes? If so, note where._____

_____

_____

Check fuse box and note the amperage and voltage._____

_____

_____

Do fuses blow? often?_____

_____

Heat

Is there sufficient heat?_____
_____
_____

Check radiators and note if the entire radiator heats up._____
_____
_____

Check radiators and note whether there are turn off handles.
_____
_____

Note if the turn handles are broken, missing or locked so that the radiator
cannot be turned on and off._____
_____
_____

Note whether the radiator leaks._____
_____
_____

DOORS

Note whether the doors close properly and securely._____
_____
_____
_____
_____
_____

Check the locks. Note if each entrance has at least one dead bolt secure lock.
(A dead bold lock cannot be picked and forces thieves who otherwise gain entrance
to the apartment to carry your personal goods out of a window which thieves don't relish
for obvious reasons.)_____
_____
_____
_____

Check and note any damage to the surfaces on both sides of each
door._____
_____
_____
_____
_____

Note if there too much space on the top, bottom or sides of any door which render the door insecure._____

_____
_____
_____
_____

Operate the door handles and note if they work and to insure that no parts are missing._____

_____
_____
_____
_____

Front Door

Note if there a peep hole for security._____

_____

Note whether there is a Fox police lock or other reinforced bar bolting the door into a plate on the floor.

KITCHEN CHECKLIST

Plumbing

Note any leaks in and under pipes and faucets._____

_____
_____
_____
_____

Note any broken handles on sinks._____

_____
_____
_____
_____

Note any chipped and pitted porcelain on sinks._____

_____
_____
_____
_____

Note whether faucets run or drip or leak._____

_____
_____
_____
_____

Is there sufficient hot water in the kitchen sink?_____

_____
_____
_____

Sink

Is there adequate water pressure?_____

_____

Is there sufficient hot and cold water?_____

_____

Is the water clean and drinkable?_____

_____
_____

Note any leaks under the drain._____

_____
_____
_____

Does water drain from the sink without problems?_____

_____

Note if the faucets are dripping, need washers or show that other visible plumbing problems exist._____

_____
_____

Note if the drains are stopped, stuffed or slow in draining water._____

_____
_____

Note if the faucets have handles and spigots that work._____

_____
_____

Check porcelain in sinks and note chips, pits, dents, discoloration and other unsightly scratches that the landlord may try to charge to your security deposit._____

_____
_____
_____
_____

Appliances

Refrigerator
Note any scratches, chips, pits, dents, discoloration or other damage to the inside or outside of the refrigerator which the landlord may try to charge to your security deposit._____

_____

_____

_____

_____

Note any missing handles, knobs, shelves, trays or doors._____

_____

_____

_____

_____

Check the inside temperature and note whether the refrigerator works and that the freezer will keep food frozen without needing the highest setting._____

_____

_____

_____

_____

Note the BTU usage in order to determine how energy efficient the refrigerator is._____

_____

_____

_____

Check door gaskets and note if the insulation is sufficient or if the gaskets need to be changed._____

_____

_____

_____

Note if the gaskets fit properly and whether they are in good condition._____

_____

_____

_____

Count and note the ice cube trays and their condition._____

_____

_____

_____

Verify and note whether all convenience items (automatic defroster, automatic ice maker and the like) are in good working order._____

_____

_____

_____

_____

Stove

Turn on each of the burners. Note whether each of the burners work._____
_____
_____
_____

Note whether the oven works._____
_____
_____

Check the inside of the oven for cleanliness, chips, dents, abrasions discoloration etc.
and note the condition.

_____
_____
_____
_____
_____

Note any damage to the inside and outside of the oven caused by cracks, dents
 chips or scratches to the porcelain. Note any stains on the inside of the oven.

_____
_____
_____
_____

Note any missing or broken handles or parts to the stove.

_____
_____
_____
_____

Verify and note whether all convenience gimmicks like the clock,
timer, etc are in good working condition._____
_____
_____
_____
_____

Insects

Look for and note evidence of infestation of roaches, mice, rats and other undesirables.

_____
_____
_____
_____

Note any mouse holes or similar holes in the walls, especially common walls into neighboring apartments._____
_____
_____
_____
_____

Obtain the name of the exterminator used by the landlord. This will usu
ally be the cheapest and most reliable exterminator you will be able to find.
Verify and note who is responsible for extermination._____
_____
_____
_____
_____

Note how often the exterminator is scheduled to come, what areas does he spray
and what pesticides does he use, because it may be hazardous to your family or your pets.
_____
_____
_____
_____
_____

Cabinets

Note any damage to the kitchen cabinets._____
_____
_____
_____
_____
_____

Note any scratches, dents, discolorations, bad or peeling paint jobs and missing handles or
shelves._____
_____
_____
_____
_____
_____

Note the condition of the hinges and whether the hinges are affixed
solidly._____
_____
_____

Note whether there sufficient cabinet space for you or will you have to add more
at your expense or at the landlord's expense.
_____

BATHROOM CHECKLIST

Sink

Note whether there is adequate water pressure in all water taps in the sinks, bathtub and shower._____

_____

_____

_____

Note whether there sufficient hot and cold water in all water taps in the sinks, bathtub and shower._____

_____

_____

_____

Note whether the water from each tap is clean and drinkable?

_____

_____

_____

_____

Check for and note leaks under the drain._____

_____

_____

Note whether the water drains from sinks and tubs without problems._____

_____

_____

_____

_____

Note whether the faucets drip, need washers or whether other visible plumbing problems exist.

_____

_____

_____

_____

Note whether the drains are stopped, stuffed or slow in draining water._____

_____

_____

_____

_____

Note whether the faucets have handles and spigots that work.

_____

_____

_____

_____

Check porcelain in sinks and tub; note chips, pits, dents, discoloration and other unsightly scratches that the landlord may try to charge to your security deposit.

_____
_____
_____
_____
_____
_____
_____

Cabinets

Note whether the bathroom cabinets are damaged._____

_____
_____
_____
_____
_____

Note any scratches, dents, discolorations, bad or peeling paint jobs and missing handles or shelves._____

_____
_____
_____
_____
_____
_____
_____
_____

Note whether there sufficient cabinet space for you or whether you have to add more at your expense._____

_____
_____
_____
_____

Bath Tub

Note whether there is adequate water pressure in all taps.

_____
_____
_____
_____

Note whether there sufficient hot and cold water in all taps.

_____
_____
_____
_____

127

Note whether the water from all taps is clean and drinkable.

_____
_____
_____
_____
_____

Note whether there are any leaks._____

_____
_____
_____

Note whether water drains from the tub without problems_____

_____
_____

Note whether the faucets drip, need washers or whether other visible plumbing problems
exist._____

_____
_____
_____
_____
_____

Note whether the drain is stopped, stuffed or slow in draining
water._____

_____
_____

Note whether the faucets have handles and spigots that work.

_____
_____
_____

Check the porcelain in the tub and note chips, pits, dents, discoloration and
other unsightly scratches that the landlord may try to charge to your security deposit

_____
_____
_____
_____
_____

Mirror

Note whether the mirror over the sink is broken, cracked or discolored._____

_____
_____
_____
_____

Note whether the mirror is blotchy and needs resilvering in
places._____

_____
_____

Note whether there a medicine cabinet and if the hinges work and their condition.

_____
_____
_____
_____
_____

Examine the medicine cabinet shelves and note rust stains, discoloration and other evidence of damage._____

_____
_____
_____
_____

Tiles

Note whether there missing, loose, cracked or unmatching bathroom tiles.

_____
_____
_____
_____
_____

Examine the grout and note mildew or evidence that new grout is necessary to hold the tiles in place._____

_____
_____
_____
_____

Commodes

Note any broken handles on commodes._____

_____
_____
_____

Note any chipped and pitted porcelain on commodes._____

_____
_____
_____

Note whether toilet runs, drips or leaks._____

_____
_____
_____

Note whether toilet flushes completely after each flush._____

_____

_____

Note whether toilet seat is securely attached._____

_____

_____

Note whether toilet seat is broken, chipped or cracked?_____

_____

_____

LIVING ROOM CHECK LIST

LIVING ROOM

Ceiling and Walls—describe any holes. State size and depth in inches or millimeters._____

_____

Describe any cracks and the length of
each._____

_____

_____

Falling
plaster_____

_____

Peeling paint_____

_____

Look for discolored yellow or brown marks indicating water leaks form the floor above and describe them._____

_____

_____

Floor—describe any holes and the size and depth of each in inches or millimeters._____

_____

_____

Note any soft spots where floor gives when stepped on._____

_____

_____

Note any significant degree of
slant._____

_____

Note any ripped or cracked linoleum or the condition of other floor covering such as carpeting or rugs._____

_____
_____
_____

Windows—Inspect glass closely.
Note any cracks, holes, or missing
glass._____

_____
_____
_____

Check window panes for loose putty and note if panes are loose in the mullions._____

_____
_____
_____
_____

Open windows and note if they slide up and down._____

_____
_____
_____

Note whether windows stay in raised position without falling.

_____
_____
_____

Inspect screens and storms for serviceability and note rips, cracks and tears etc.

_____

_____
_____

Note whether there a lock on the window and does it
work?_____

_____
_____
_____

Is there a fire escape and how secure is it for escape and to keep out intruders?_____

_____
_____

Check windows for drafts._____

_____
_____

Electrical—Count the number of electrical outlets. Verify and note whether they work._____

_____
_____

Do all light switches work?_____

_____

_____

Is there unwrapped and exposed wiring in contravention of building codes? If so, note
where._____

_____

_____

Heat
Is there sufficient heat?_____

_____

_____

Check radiators and note if the entire radiator heats up._____

_____

_____

Check radiators and note whether there are turn off handles.

_____

_____

Note if the turn handles broken, missing or locked so that the radiator
cannot be turned on and off._____

_____

_____

Note whether the radiator leaks._____

_____

_____

Telephone Jacks

Note whether there enough telephone Jacks in conveniently located
places._____

_____

_____

_____

BEDROOM CHECK LIST

BED ROOM

Ceiling and Walls—describe any holes. State size and depth in inches or millimeters._____

_____

Describe any cracks and the length of each._____

_____
_____
_____

Falling plaster_____

_____

Peeling paint_____

_____

Look for discolored yellow or brown marks indicating water leaks form the floor above and describe them._____

_____
_____

Floor—describe any holes and the size and depth of each in inches or millimeters._____

_____
_____

Note any soft spots where floor gives when stepped on._____

_____
_____

Note any significant degree of slant._____

_____
_____

Note any ripped or cracked linoleum or the condition of other floor covering such as carpeting or rugs._____

_____
_____

Windows—Inspect glass closely.

Note any cracks, holes, or missing glass._____
_____
_____
_____

Check window panes for loose putty and note if panes are loose in the
mullions._____
_____
_____
_____

Open windows and note if they slide up and down._____
_____
_____
_____

Note whether windows stay in raised position without falling.
_____
_____
_____

Inspect screens and storms for serviceability and note rips, cracks and tears etc.
_____
_____
_____

Note whether there is a lock on the window and does it work?
_____
_____
_____

Is there a fire escape and how secure is it for escape and to keep out intruders?
_____
_____
_____

Check windows for drafts._____
_____
_____

Electrical—Count the number of electrical outlets. Verify and note whether they work.
_____
_____
_____

Do all light switches work?_____
_____
_____

Is there unwrapped and exposed wiring in contravention of building codes? If so, note where._____

_____

_____

Heat

Is there sufficient heat?_____

_____

_____

Check radiators and note if the entire radiator heats up._____

_____

_____

Check radiators and note whether there are turn off handles.

_____

_____

Note if the turn handles broken, missing or locked so that the radiator cannot be turned on and off._____

_____

_____

Note whether the radiator leaks._____

_____

_____

Telephone Jacks

Note whether there enough telephone Jacks in conveniently located places.

_____

_____

_____

_____

_____

MISCELLANEOUS

Verify that the Heat and Air Conditioning in each room is suitable to your needs and note any deficiencies in their operating systems or housings.

_____
_____
_____
_____
_____
_____
_____
_____

Note whether all telephone jacks in the residence are working.

_____
_____

Note whether there are trash bins and the days of rubbish removal. Also not whether refuse must be recycled. Note who removes trash and the cost to you, if any.

_____
_____
_____
_____

Note the condition of the closet space including whether the bars for hanging clothes are securely affixed to the wall on each side.

_____
_____
_____
_____

Note whether there is a storage bin in the basement that comes with the dwelling. Note the cost to you, if any. Note the condition of the bin and any apparent damage to the bin._____

_____
_____
_____

Determine and note whether utilities are included in the rent or mu st you pay the electric, gas and water bill directly to the utility.

_____
_____
_____
_____
_____
_____

Get estimates as to the monthly cost of each of the utilities and note the estimated cost of each._____

_____
_____
_____
_____
_____
_____

Note whether there separate gas, electric and water meters for each apartment.
If not, verify and note how the landlord apportions the bills.

_____
_____
_____
_____
_____
_____

Check the overall layout of the floor plan of the residence.
Note the size of each room from the floor plan in width and length.

_____
_____
_____
_____
_____
_____

Try to get a fix on the amount of noise audible in the dwelling from outside sources.
Open the windows and note the noise level.
Note the condition of carpets which insulate the
noise._____

_____
_____
_____
_____
_____

Is there a laundry on the premises?   Is it run by the landlord or the tenants.
Note the cost, the hours of operation and the arrangements.

_____
_____
_____
_____
_____

Note whether there a parking lot in the building and a space allocated for your car.
Note the monthly charges. Note where guests park. What if you are a two car family?

_____
_____
_____
_____
_____

Note whether there is a master antenna on the roof with which you can hook up.
Note whether the building is wired for cable TV and the cost of any hook-ups.

_____

_____

_____

_____

Note whether the building has a health club, swimming pool, sauna or other amenities.
Note the fee or charge to use the facilities.

_____

_____

_____

_____

_____

Note whether there is a doorman and note his duties. _____
Note the special services the door man provides and the hours he is in attendance.

_____

_____

_____

_____

Note the security arrangements surrounding the dwelling.
Note whether each residence has a peep hole viewer in the front door, a smoke alarm,
fire extinguisher, chain lock on the front door, dead bolt locks, Fox floor to door police
locks and reliable guards._____

_____

_____

_____

_____

_____

_____

Note whether each room has a radiator or heat vent._____

_____

_____

_____

_____

Note whether each room has an air conditioner or vent._____

_____

_____

_____

_____

A REMINDER

Don't forget to take pictures of any pre-existing damage to the residence.

LIST OF GOALS AND PRIORITIES FORM

LIST OF GOALS	PRIORITY OF EACH GOAL	DOLLAR VALUE OF EACH GOAL
1.		
2.		
3.		
4.		
5.		
6.		

TENANT'S OFFER SHEET

PREMISES LOCATED AT_____

_____

_____

DATE: _____

NAME OF LANDLORD OR AGENT_____

RENT

FIRST
 OFFER   COUNTER-OFFER

SECOND
 OFFER   COUNTER-OFFER

THIRD
 OFFER   COUNTER-OFFER

CONCESSIONS

FIRST
 OFFER   COUNTER-OFFER

SECOND
 OFFER   COUNTER-OFFER

THIRD
 OFFER   COUNTER-OFFER

_____
Landlord

_____
Tenant

TENANT'S SECURITY DEPOSIT CLAUSE

Landlord agrees to hold tenant's security deposit as trust funds in a segregated interest bearing bank account and to inform tenant of the name and address of the bank where the account is maintained within the next thirty days.

Landlord shall return the security deposit to tenant with all accrued interest when the lease shall have terminated, provided that Tenant has substantially complied with the lease. Landlord may keep one percent of the accrued interest as an administrative fee.

At the end of this lease landlord agrees to render an itemized list of deductions, if any, for damage landlord claims tenant has caused to the premises.

Landlord recognizes that tenant needs the prompt return of the security deposit to use as rent for tenant's next dwelling. Accordingly landlord agrees to return the security deposit or the unused portion thereof to the tenant at the same time that the tenant surrenders the keys to the dwelling to the landlord.

RECEIPT FOR SECURITY DEPOSIT

RECEIVED from_____

Insert name of Tenant(s) as in the lease

the Sum of $_____

Insert amount of security deposit

as a security deposit in connection with the lease of premises known as

_____

Insert street address of the dwelling

_____.

Insert city, state and zip code of the dwelling

The security deposit shall be returned with all accrued interest when the lease shall terminate, provided that Tenant(s) have substantially complied with the lease. Landlord may keep one percent of the accrued rent as an administrative fee.

Signed _____

Insert name of landlord or agent

RECEIPT FOR ADVANCE RENT

RECEIVED From_____
Insert your name

The Sum of $_____
Insert amount of advance rent

as _____ month's (weeks) of advance
Insert number of month's/weeks advance rent

rent in connection with premises known as_____ _

_____.
Insert street, city and zip code address of the dwelling

The advance rent shall be applied to the initial month(s) of the lease.

Signed_____
Insert name of landlord or agent

TENANT'S CONCESSIONS CLAUSE

Landlord hereby agrees to grant the following concessions to Tenant at landlord's expense:

1._____
Insert concessions, i.e., number of month's free rent, air conditioning unit, new paint job, quality of materials,
etc.

2._____

3._____

4._____

TENANT'S WORK ORDER CLAUSE

Landlord agrees to complete for the tenant the work set forth below. Landlord shall use all best efforts to complete the work prior to tenant's move -in date. Landlord agrees that all work on the premises will be completed not later that 30 days after tenant's move-in date.
Landlord agrees to use materials equal to builders' standard
unless a higher quality or brand name is set forth below.

Landlord agrees to perform <u>at landlord's expense</u> the work set forth below:

(Insert itemized list of work to be performed and the quality of materials to be used).

1.

2.

3.

4.

Landlord agrees to perform <u>at tenant's expense</u> the work set forth below:
(Insert itemized list of work to be performed and the quality of materials to be used).

1.

2.

3.

4.

LANDLORD VITAL INFORMATION SHEET

FOR YOUR INFORMATION:
IMPORTANT TELEPHONE NUMBERS

Landlord's name _____

Landlord's address _____

_____

Landlord's business phone number_____
Landlord's home phone number_____

Police Department_____
Fire Department_____
 Ambulance_____
Paramedic Service_____
 Doctor_____
Telephone Company_____
Gas Company_____
Electric Company_____
Water Company_____
Cable TV Company_____
Garbage Removal_____
 Exterminator_____

Building Manager_____
 Landlord_____
 Janitor_____
Doorman_____
 Plumber_____
 Electrician_____

Location of the fire extinguisher nearest your dwelling:

_____

Location of the main electrical shutoff for your dwelling:

_____

Location of the main gas shutoff valve for your dwelling:

_____

Location of the main water shutoff for your dwelling:

_____

Location of garbage and refuse removal cans:

_____

Miscellaneous:

_____

_____

_____

_____

TENANT'S MOVE-IN CLAUSE

If tenant shall notify landlord in writing of tenant's decision not to take possession or move into the rented premises prior to the designated effective date or move-in date, Tenant's liability shall be limited to

_____

Insert number month's rent.

TENANT'S COOLING OFF PERIOD CLAUSE

It is expressly agreed between landlord and tenant that notwithstanding any provision in this lease to the contrary, tenant shall have the right to reject this lease for _____ business days after

Insert number of days

the execution and delivery of this lease by tenant. Should tenant exercise this right of rejection, this lease shall be null and void and of no legal significance with the same force and effect as if never signed by the tenant.

All moneys paid by the tenant hereunder shall immediately be returned by landlord to tenant.

DELIVERY OF THE PREMISES CLAUSE

If the landlord is unable to deliver occupancy of the premises to the tenant on the move-in day or other commencement date of the lease, the landlord shall at tenant's option immediatedly return to tenant all of the moneys previously paid by tenant hereunder.

It is the express understanding of the landlord and tenant that tenant needs premises in which to live.

Accordingly, should landlord for any reason be unable to deliver the premises to tenant, landlord will immediately return all such moneys to tenant so that tenant can find other housing.

Tenant's obligation to pay rent shall begin when tenant actually receives possession of the premises.

TENANT'S RENT RECEIPT FORM

date: _____

RECEIVED This day from_____
Insert Your Name

the sum of $_____ as rent for premises known as
Insert the Amount Paid

_____
Insert the Address and Apartment Number

for the period beginning_____
Insert the First Day for which Rent Was Paid

and ending_____
Insert the Last Day for which Rent Was Paid

or for the month (week) of _____
Insert Month or Week

_____
Signed

_____
Title

TENANT'S ASSIGNMENT CLAUSE

Tenant shall have the right to assign this lease subject to the written consent of the landlord. Landlord agrees not to unreasonably withhold consent to such assignment. Any assignee with a net worth and credit standing equal to or in excess of the tenant's shall presumptively be deemed to be an acceptable assignee.

Any assignment hereunder shall be effective _____ days after the tenant shall have notified.
        Insert Number of Days

The landlord of the proposed assignment along with a copy of the proposed assignee's net worth statement and Consumer Credit Report. In the event of any such assignment, the original tenant shall be released from the lease and a novation shall be deemed to have occurred.

TENANT'S FORM OF ASSIGNMENT

For value received the undersigned, as tenant under a certain
lease, between the undersigned and _____

_____
        Insert name and address of landlord

_____,

as landlord, relating to premises situate and known as

_____
        Insert address of premises to be assigned

_____

_____

(the "premises") hereby assigns all of the right, title and interest in and to the lease
of the undersigned for the premises to

_____
        Insert name and address of person(s) to whom the lease is to be assigned

_____

_____

TENANT'S SUBLEASE CLAUSE

Tenant shall have the right to sublease the premises subject to the written consent of the landlord . Landlord agrees not to unreasonably withhold consent to such subleasing. Any sublease with a net worth and credit standing equal to or in excess of the tenant's shall presumptively be deemed to be an acceptable tenant.

Any sublease hereunder shall be effective _____ days after the tenant shall have notified

Insert number

landlord of the proposed sublease along with (i) a copy of the proposed assignee's net worth statement, (ii) a copy of the proposes assignee's Consumer Credit Report, (iii) the written consent of any cotenant or guarantor of the lease and (iv) a copy of the proposed sublease.

NOTE THAT YOU WILL NEED A PROPOSED SUBLEASE. **LEASE ON YOUR TERMS** SUGGESTS THAT YOU START WITH A PHOTOCOPY OF YOUR LEASE. WHITE WASH OUT THE NAMES AND ADDRESSES OF THE LANDLORD AND TENANT. REPLACE THOSE NAMES AND ADDRESSES WITH YOUR NAME AND NEW ADDRESS AS LANDLORD AND THE PROPOSED SUBTENANT'S NAME AS TENANT.

NOTICE OF ENTRY

Dear Tenant:

RE: ADVANCE NOTICE OF ENTRY

Reference is made to premises situate at

_____

_____

Insert tenant's address

_____   _____.

Please take notice that the landlord or his designee intends to enter your premises on

_____199__

Insert date

at or about_____(AM) (PM)

for the purpose of_____

_____

Insert purpose of entry

_____

It is anticipated that they will stay approximately_____ (Hours : Minutes).

Insert amount of time

Your presence is not necessary unless otherwise stated herein. Should you not be available to open the door, a pass key will be used for entry.

Thank you for your cooperation.

_____

Landlord

148

NOTICE OF SHUT DOWN OF SERVICES

Dear Tenant:

       RE: NOTICE OF SHUT DOWN OF SERVICES

       DATE:_____

Reference is made to premises situate at _____

_____

       Insert address and unit number

_____.

Please take notice that there will be a curtailment of services as set forth below:

DATE AND TIME _____

NATURE OF SERVICE(S)_____

_____

_____

ANTICIPATED DURATION OF OUTAGE_____(DAYS) (HOURS)

_____
      Landlord

TENANT'S REPAIRS CLAUSE

Landlord shall be responsible for all repairs to the dwelling.

TENANT'S NOTICE OF DEFECT LETTER

_____
Insert date

Re: Notice of Defect

_____
Insert name of landlord or agent

_____
Insert street address of landlord

_____
Insert city, state and zip code

Dear Landlord:

This will confirm the conversation we had today concerning defects in and necessary repair(s) to the dwelling of the undersigned. As you were informed, the following work needs to be done:

_____
Itemize repairs that must be made.

_____

_____

_____

I am relying upon you to make the repairs in a reasonable time and before further damage and possible harm can occur.

Very truly yours,

_____
Insert your name

_____
Insert your street address

_____
Insert your city, state, zip code

TENANT'S FOLLOW UP NOTICE LETTER

_____
Insert date

Re: Landlord's failure to repair

_____
Insert name of landlord or agent

_____
Insert landlord's street address

_____
Insert landlord's city, state and zip code

Dear Landlord:

Reference is made to my prior communications to you concerning defects in and necessary repairs to my residence. You will recall that the following repairs must be made in order to make my residence habitable (Insert an itemized list of necessary repairs) :

_____
_____
_____
_____
_____
_____
_____

The situation is getting worse by the passage of time and is bound to deteriorate even further. In the meantime, my standard of living is eroding and my physical security is imperiled.
The provisions of my lease with you and applicable state and local law require you to effectuate repairs. I do not know what to do next. However, I would like to know that my rent payments will be used to keep my residence in good repair and to prevent injury to me, my family and the general public.
If I do not hear from you presently, I shall have to take whatever action is necessary in order to pursue all of my rights.

    Very Truly Yours,

_____
Insert your name

_____
Insert your street address

_____
Insert your city, state and zip code

TENANT'S INSURANCE CLAUSE

Tenant shall maintain casualty insurance coverage of at least $100,000 per occurrence.

TENANT'S NOTICES CLAUSE

Notices required to by given under this lease shall be delivered by personal service or sent certified mail, return receipt requested, with a second copy sent by ordinary first class mail in a postage prepaid, properly addressed envelope.
Notices shall be deemed effective when actually received.

TENANT'S PROPERTY TAX REBATE CLAUSE

Landlord agrees to provide a pro rata tax rebate to the tenant for each year in which the landlord receives a property tax reduction. Tenant's pro rata share of the property tax reduction shall be based upon the ratio which the number of square feet of tenant's dwelling bears to the total number of rentable square feet in the total building.

Landlord shall recoup all of the reasonable and necessary legal fees spent in obtaining the property tax rebate and shall only share with tenant the net amount of the property tax rebate after deducting such legal fees.

TENANT'S NO LESS FAVORABLE LEASE RENEWAL CLAUSE

Landlord agrees that any renewal lease with tenant will contain no less favorable terms and conditions than the terms and conditions of this lease except for changes in the rent.

TENANT'S MOST FAVORED NATIONS CLAUSE

Landlord agrees that the rent on renewal of this lease shall be no higher than the lowest rent charged by landlord to any other tenant in the building in which the premises is located for a comparable unit during the sixty days immediately preceding the expiry of this lease. This formula may be applied on the basis of rent per square foot in the building, if no comparable unit exists.

TENANT'S HOLDOVER CLAUSE

If tenant gives notice of his intention to quit the premises and does not deliver up possession at the time specified in such notice or otherwise becomes a holdover tenant, tenant shall continue to pay the same rent at the same time and in the same manner as otherwise payable hereunder so long as tenant shall continue in possession.

TENANT'S MITIGATION OF DAMAGES CLAUSE

Landlord agrees at the end of this lease to take all reasonable steps necessary to show tenant's premises to all new prospective tenants in order to mitigate tenant's liabilities hereunder.

TENANT'S REMOVAL OF FIXTURES AND IMPROVEMENTS CLAUSE

When this lease ends, Tenant may remove all fixtures, installations or attachments which tenant has placed at any time in or on the premises.

TENANT'S NO SELF-HELP CLAUSE

Landlord agrees not to resort to the remedy of self-help in the event of an alleged or purported breach of this lease by Tenant. It is the express understanding of the tenant and the landlord that all controversies arising from this lease be resolved by negotiation between the parties or by courts of competent jurisdiction.

TENANT'S NO DISTRAINT CLAUSE

Landlord hereby waives any right of distraint or other like remedy landlord may have at common law, by state or local law, or otherwise under this lease.

TENANT'S NO SECURITY INTEREST CLAUSE

Landlord acknowledges that landlord takes no grant of a security interest in any of the tenant's personal property. Landlord hereby renounces any such security interest which landlord may otherwise have.

TENANT'S NO CONFESSION OF JUDGMENT CLAUSE

Notwithstanding anything else to the contrary herein or elsewhere, this lease shall not be deemed to have any confessions of judgment in it in favor of any party. No party to this lease intends to or has confessed judgment on any matter relating to this lease.

TENANT'S EXEMPT PROPERTY CLAUSE

No security interest or pledge is granted by tenant to landlord of tenant's personal property exempt by law from levy and sale by virtue of an execution. Landlord expressly waives and renounces any clause in the printed lease contrary hereto.

LETTER TO BETTER BUSINESS BUREAU

Better Business Bureau

_____

Insert street address

_____

Insert city, state and zip code

_____

Insert date

RE: PURCHASE OF MOBILE HOME OR HOMESITE

Gentlemen:

I am currently considering a purchase of a mobile home or lease of a mobile homesite from the dealer or business set forth below:

_____

Insert name of business

_____

Insert street address of business

_____

Insert city, state and zip code

Would you please advise as to whether there are any complaints on file with your organization against that vendor.

Very truly yours,

_____

Insert your name

_____

Insert your street address

_____

Insert your city, state, and zip code

TENANT'S DEFINITIONS CLAUSE

For purposes of these riders _____

Insert name(s) of tenant(s)

shall be referred to individually and collectively as the "tenant",

and _____

Insert name of landlord

shall be referred to as the "landlord".

These definitional terms of tenant and landlord shall be deemed to mesh and be read in context with whatever definitional terms each party may have in the main body of the lease.

TENANT'S RIDER INCLUSION CLAUSE

It is agreed between the landlord and the tenant that the Tenant's Riders to this lease be and hereby are deemed to be part of this lease with the same force and effect as if set forth in their entirety in the pre-printed body of the lease.

TENANT'S SUPREMACY CLAUSE

The riders to this lease shall be deemed to supplement the original text of the landlord's form of lease when both clauses are in agreement.

In the case of conflict the terms of the riders shall be deemed to override and supersede the terms of the original landlord's form of lease. The intent of the parties to this lease is that the tenant has bargained for and otherwise paid for the inclusion of these riders and should receive the benefit of the rights contained in the riders to this lease.

TENANT'S WARRANTY OF HABITABILITY CLAUSE

All of the sections of this lease are subject to the provisions of a warranty of habitability expressly made by landlord to tenant. Nothing in this lease shall be interpreted to mean that tenant has waived any rights concerning the warranty of habitability. Landlord agrees that the residence and the common areas are fit for human habitation and that there are no conditions which are or will be suffered to be detrimental to life, health or safety.

TENANT'S LEGAL FEES CLAUSE

If either party to this lease shall bring any cause of action or proceeding against the other party for enforcement of this lease, the prevailing party shall recover reasonable and necessary legal fees and expenses from the loosing party.

TENANT'S RIGHT TO A JURY TRIAL CLAUSE

Nothing contained in this lease or otherwise shall constitute a waiver of the right to a trial by jury in a court action, proceeding or counterclaim on any matters concerning this lease, the relationship of the parties as landlord and tenant, or the tenant's use and occupancy of the dwelling.

TENANT'S GRACE PERIOD CLAUSE

Tenant shall have a seven business day grace period in which to cure any default under this lease. The seven day grace period shall commence upon the day that the landlord delivers written notice to the tenant of the alleged default.

EXCULPATORY CLAUSES SHALL BE DEEMED VOID

Landlord and tenant agree that any clause in this lease attempting to exculpate the landlord from landlord's own negligence or misconduct shall be deemed null and void.

TENANT'S LIQUIDATED DAMAGES CLAUSE

Landlord agrees that tenant's damages hereunder for unpaid rent shall be limited to $_____.
Nothing herein shall limit tenant's liability for (i) physical damage to the premises
or (ii) for reimbursement of landlord's reasonable and actual legal fees and expenses.

Insert amount

TENANT'S RELEASE FORM

In consideration of the sum of ten dollars and other good and valuable consideration the receipt of which is hereby acknowledged, the undersigned landlord and tenant hereby release each other from any and all claims that each had or may have had against the other arising from a certain lease between them.

_____
Insert name of landlord

_____
Insert name of tenant

_____
Insert date

Sworn to before me this

_____ day of _____, 199__

_____
Notary Public

_____
Seal.

159

TENANT'S NOTICE OF INTENTION TO VACATE FORM

To: _____
    Insert name of landlord

    _____
    Insert street address of landlord

    _____
    Insert landlord's city, state and zip code

Date:_____
     Insert date notice is given

Re: Tenant's notice of intention to vacate premises
Reference is made to premises known as_____

_____
        Insert address of premises

_____ .

Please take notice that the undersigned tenant(s) will vacate the premises
on_____ .
        Insert date you intend to move out

In accordance with the lease the tenant's security deposit should be returned

_____
        Set forth the return date for your security deposit

_____

Please forward mail to the following forwarding address:

_____
        Insert your new forwarding address

_____

_____

        _____
                        Tenant

        _____
                        Tenant

    Mailed certified mail return receipt requested with a second copy mailed first class mail in a postage
prepaid properly addressed envelope; or Delivered by Hand:

RECEIVED_____
                Landlord or agent

    Date:_____

NOTES

NOTES

NOTES

NOTES